# The Cross of St Andrew

# The Cross of St Andrew

## Ursula Hall

BIRLINN

First published in 2006 by
Birlinn Limited
West Newington House
10 Newington Road
Edinburgh
EH9 1QS

*www.birlinn.co.uk*

ISBN 10: 1 84158 518 1
ISBN 13: 978 1 84158 518 5

British Library Cataloguing-in-Publication Data
A catalogue record for this book is available from the British Library

Typeset by Iolaire Typesetting, Newtonmore
Printed and bound by Cromwell Press Ltd, Trowbridge, Wiltshire

# Contents

# List of Illustrations

# List of Plates

# *Foreword*

This book has its origin in the surprise I felt when I was working on the cult of St Andrew the Apostle in Scotland and I discovered that the association of the saint with the X-shaped cross – the cross from which the Scottish flag, the saltire, derives – is not a feature in the early cult of St Andrew and does not appear in any of the apocryphal material describing his martyrdom.

The chapters that follow are a record of my attempt to use both the literary and the iconographical evidence to determine when and where this development in the popular tradition and in the depiction of St Andrew's death might have taken place, and to put before myself and my readers some speculative ideas to explain how it could have happened.

I have tried to treat these detailed and sometimes difficult subjects in a way that the general reader will find interesting and straightforward, and I have not burdened the text with many notes and references. I believe the bibliography will provide sufficient guidance for those who want to follow up or challenge my evidence and my conclusions.

I have had to venture into aspects of religious and philoso-phical thinking, and of iconographical investigation, with its possibilities and pitfalls, where I know myself to be no more than an interested amateur. I hope, however, that scholars in the various fields involved in a study like this will consider the questions I have raised and be able to elaborate and firm up some of my arguments, perhaps rule out others, and above all develop new productive lines of research.

Many individuals and institutions have helped me in this investigation. I should like to thank the numerous friends and the members of my own family who have given assistance with the preparation of the text, who have contributed ideas and valuable questions, and have given me fruitful leads to relevant St Andrew images and academic publications. I owe particular debts to Aldyth Cadoux, Elaine Fantham, Kenneth Fraser, Maria-José and Bob Friedlander, Christine Gascoigne, Simon Taylor, Mark Wallace and Jacqueline and Michael Wilson. I have benefited from exchanges of correspondence with several scholars in religious and iconographical studies. The text of course remains entirely my responsibility.

I should like to thank especially the people I have dealt with at the cathedrals of Canterbury, Durham, Rochester, Wells, Worcester and York; at the churches of Greystoke, Langtoft and Ludlow; at St Andrews University Library, the British Library, the Bibliothèque de l'Arsenal and the Bibliothèque Nationale in Paris, the Glencairn Museum in Bryn Athyn, USA, the British Museum and the Victoria and Albert Museum in London, and the staff of the National Trust at Laycock Abbey and of Historic Scotland at St Andrews Cathedral.

Special thanks are also due to Andrew Simmons, of Birlinn Ltd. He has overseen the book's production with efficiency and good humour, and with sympathetic consideration of the author's concerns.

Passages from Greek and Latin have all been translated by myself, and the securing of illustrative material has been a rewarding, if in some instances difficult, task, for which I acknowledge generous financial help from 'The Drummond Trust' (3 Pitt Terrace, Stirling) and 'The Strathmartine Trust' (2 Kinburn Place, St Andrews).

I dedicate this book to the memory of Christine Wolfe of St Andrews University Library, who was responsible in the first place for getting me interested in St Andrew and his puzzling cross.

Ursula Hall
St Andrews
July 2006

# I

## *The Story of St Andrew*

# 1

# *His Life*

Stories of the saints have played a big part in the life and thinking of the Christian Church. They have provided the themes for sermons, inspiration for artists, comfort and encouragement for the faithful, and unifying ideas for communities and nations. But where did the stories come from? How far back can we trace them? How much reliance can we place on them? How far could they reflect a historical reality, or, if not that, a probability or at least a possibility, as to the life and character of a real person?

On the other hand, should we rather see these stories as expressing not so much the experience of a particular individual, but the vicissitudes and aspirations of the early Church in general, and the ideas which its leaders and champions wished to put before the Christian faithful to strengthen that faith through times of persecution? And how far do they derive from the attempts of proponents of particular views, or early known 'heresies', to challenge orthodoxy? Are we dealing here not so much with history as with an entirely understandable propaganda?

A final question, however, for us, and for the purposes of this book, must be, how much does all this really *matter*, since what determined the way a saint was thought about and was actually portrayed was what people came to believe about him, not what they could possibly know.

When we look at these stories, especially those relating to the original disciples of Jesus, living and dying in the first century AD, we have to ask ourselves how any such stories could have been preserved and spread around in the long period when the Church had to operate largely under cover, and at times its members were fiercely harassed, before the ending of persecution by the 'Edict of Milan' in AD 313, under the Emperor Constantine. We must be prepared to accept that, even if we decide that there may be a core of truth in them, differing motivations and influences might have been at work affecting the tradition over these years, and also that there was strong pressure to provide some sort of detailed story for every important saint if the tradition itself was very thin.

The New Testament as we have it dates back to the second half of the second century AD, but papyrus fragments and other evidence show that some of its material was circulating widely much earlier. The book of Acts gives a lot of information about the early Church, and of the spreading of the gospel by some of the disciples, and especially by the Apostle Paul. Although there are many sceptical academics who question much of this account, I would myself join those who believe the events narrated and the people portrayed probably do give a basically reliable picture of those formative and exciting years.

However, we are concerned with St Andrew, and it has to be said at once that in Acts nothing is told about him, about what he was doing, in this period. In the Gospels he had indeed appeared as an individual, brother of Simon Peter, and one of the twelve disciples close to Jesus. In the Gospel of St John more is said of him; he is more of a personality. Here we are told that Andrew was a follower of John the Baptist, and having met Jesus through him he went to his brother Simon and said 'We have found the Messiah'. (It is for this reason that St Andrew is often described, especially in Byzantine-Orthodox tradition, as the 'first-called' – with all that implies in terms of comparison with the other apostles, even St Peter.) He played a significant part in two incidents that are described later in the Gospel of St John. But beyond that, in our Bible, there is nothing.

Apart from the writings that were accepted to make up our New Testament, there were however many accounts of the lives and martyrdoms of the apostles circulating in the early Church, and considerable parts of these texts, or of versions thought to depend on them, survive, and can be studied in collections of what are called the New Testament Apocrypha.

This material has come down to us in the form of brief

references in the texts of the Church fathers, and of passages incorporated in the Church liturgy, especially for the services celebrating the festival days of the various saints, and in manuscripts in many different languages, manuscripts which are themselves copies of copies of copies, made over the centuries, with all that must mean in terms of additions, omissions and mistakes. From these sources scholars attempt to reconstruct the version of the *Acta* (literally, the *Doings*) of the saints that would have been circulating in the early Church. There is enough material to get back to substantial accounts of the activities of five, St Peter, St Andrew, St John, St Paul and St Thomas, written in the late second or early third century AD.

Even so, what we get is something very far removed from contemporary biography, and we have to bear in mind that in the early Church itself there was much doubt as to the reliability of certain *Acta*. Some were condemned, for example by St Augustine, as work contaminated by heretical beliefs, and some were put on a papal 'black list', not to be read by the faithful. Obviously a certain sifting out went on, and an orthodox account of the life and martyrdom of each saint came to be accepted. It was this story which was told in the churches, and came to be put into writing and circulated among the reading public, both clerical and lay. Whether it represented what had actually happened was another matter. It is not being unduly cynical to say that historical truth was regarded as of less importance than the value of the story as exemplifying and encouraging the Christian life.

And alongside this 'official' account there still survived remnants of other, often more fantastical, tales, tales of exciting adventures in strange lands against strange enemies. These were perhaps more fun to tell and to read than any record of actual facts, the approved accounts of the steady and devoted spreading of the gospel through the Roman Empire, in the face of all too ordinary hardships, and what might be described as 'routine' opposition and persecution.

Some of these points will be illustrated if we now come to look at the ancient evidence relating to the life and death of our subject, St Andrew. In doing this we shall also be able to consider whether, in spite of all that I have written above, we may be able to find a core of historical truth, or at least probability, in the traditions about him, as in the traditions about some of the other apostles.

Eusebius, Bishop of Caesarea and friend of Emperor Constantine the Great, wrote in his *History of the Church*, of about AD 324, that, 'when the holy apostles and disciples of our Saviour were dispersed through the whole world, tradition tells us that the lot sent Thomas to Parthia, while Scythia was allotted to Andrew, and Asia [= western Turkey, around Ephesus] to John' (*Hist. Eccl.* 3.1). This information is thought to have come from the Christian writer Origen, who died about AD 254.

By 'Scythia' we should probably understand the lands around and to the north of the Black Sea. There is some apocryphal material that tells of Andrew's adventures along the southern shores of that sea, and some that has him journeying there together with his brother Peter.

A writer of the ninth century AD, Epiphanius, says that in his own researches into the history of St Andrew he went to Sinope (= modern Sinop, on the Turkish Black Sea coast). There he was shown by an aged monk an oratory, with, the monk claimed, the ancient thrones from which Peter and Andrew had preached and the stone beds where they had slept. There was also surviving an 'ancient representation of Andrew himself taken from life' (*PG* 120, col. 129) – a painting, I think, is meant, rather than a statue – which had miraculously escaped destruction by the iconoclasts. (The iconoclastic movement was strong in the eighth century, and was based on opposition to 'the worship of images'. It led to much destruction, as the comparable movement in our own Reformation did.)

Epiphanius appears to have been a pretty gullible tourist taken advantage of by the locals in Sinope, but it seems to me that there is nothing implausible about the idea that Andrew, many centuries earlier, could have travelled in these parts. Around the Black Sea there were civilised communities both within and beyond the Roman Empire, with established cultural and trading connections with the Mediterranean world, and often including a substantial Jewish element in their populations. It would have been a natural area for the spreading of the gospel.

It should be noted, in fact, that Sinope itself was an important developed city in the first century AD, favoured by the Romans since the time of Caesar with colonial status. It was situated in the Roman province of Bithynia-Pontus where one of the most famous governors was Pliny the Younger, around AD 112. We have surviving some of Pliny's correspondence with the Emperor Trajan, in which one of the problems discussed is how to deal with Christians in the province (*Epistulae* 10, 96 and 97). This date falls only two or at most three generations after that of possible proselytising by Andrew or another apostle.

There is a great deal of material which is to be thought of as dependent in a sense on this geographical tradition connecting Andrew with the Black Sea. In manuscripts of many different languages, including Greek, Latin, Syriac and Coptic, there are related Andrew's adventures in the land of 'Mermidonia', of 'cannibals', or of 'dogs', which in most sources seems to be located in 'Scythia' – in the Crimea or southern Russia. Andrew is sent there to rescue another apostle, Matthias or Matthew, and the story is one of miraculous escapes and dramatic heavenly interventions.

A version of this colourful tale of particular interest to us is one in Old English, the *Andreas*, which is included in the *Vercelli Book*. This is a collection of Anglo-Saxon prose and verse texts in a manuscript written in AD 950–1000 and found in the chapter archives of the Cathedral of Vercelli in north Italy. The *Andreas*, which is available in modern English, is an interesting read, both for the story itself with, among other things, its account of cannibalism, and for the way in which doctrinal points are made. It seems in fact to have been a serious work, written by a serious poet with strong theological interests.

However, many versions of these adventures were less worthy; they seem to have been sensationalist and unedifying from the Christian point of view, and would not have been favoured by the Church authorities. This accounts for the fact that they have not much affected the general tradition about St Andrew, and these adventures were not very often illustrated in the iconography of the saint. An example, actually in Britain, is in the stained glass of the east window of Greystoke Church, near Penrith. Unfortunately, the detailed interpretation of the scenes is very difficult here, because of clumsy restoration.

1. St Andrew arrives in the land of the cannibals. From east window of St Andrew's Church, Greystoke, Penrith (Photo: Canon D. Ellis)

A further development of the Andrew story that builds on the connection with the Black Sea area is the tradition that he travelled to Georgia, and also to Kiev, in the Ukraine. Indeed, an eleventh/twelfth-century Russian chronicle has Andrew not only founding the church in Kiev, but even going as far as Novgorod, well on the way to the Baltic!

Another tradition credits Andrew with the establishment of Christianity in the great city of Byzantium (long before it became 'Constantinople' of course), and the consecration of the first bishop there. This particular aspect of the story is generally regarded as a late addition to the original Andrew *Acta*, and to be due to the wish of the Church in the East to claim great antiquity for their line of bishops. They wanted to associate this with St Andrew in a way that would strengthen their claims to parity, or even priority, compared with Rome and the Church there, established by Andrew's brother, St Peter.

There are some texts that place Andrew's death in the East; for example, there is an Arabic version of a Coptic (Egyptian Christian) original which said that Andrew spread the gospel among the 'Kurds', and then died, on the cross, at Lydda in Israel. However, these are not fully fleshed-out stories, and in those accounts of Andrew's eastern adventures that I have been writing about, in Asia Minor and Scythia, it is not said that he actually suffered martyrdom anywhere in these parts. Indeed in most of the texts there is explicit reference to the continuation of his travels, to Greece, and to eventual death at Patras. The story of his crucifixion at Patras became the universally accepted end, the climax, of his life of Christian commitment.

As I have said, little is made in the dominant accounts of St Andrew's life, at least in our Western tradition, of the stories about the rescue of Matthias/Matthew, and the struggle to convert cannibals to Christianity. The Church naturally favoured the emphasis on Andrew's missionary work in Greece, and on the events leading up to his death. There are several accounts of this, and I shall discuss them in detail later when I come to write about the way in which Andrew's martyrdom is described in ancient sources.

At this point I want to bring into our picture of the St Andrew tradition the work of Gregory of Tours. St Gregory lived from AD 538 to 594, and he wrote a number of works, most importantly a *History of the Franks*, which is a vital source for the student of early European history. He also wrote (in Latin, of course) a *Book of St Andrew's Miracles*. He says that he has a special affection for the saint, as he was himself born on 30 November, the feast day of St Andrew. In his prologue he writes that, whereas in the case of most of the saints all that survives is an account of their passion or martyrdom, in the case of St Andrew he has come across the detailed story of his miraculous deeds and virtues. He proposes to write a selective version of this work, hoping that it 'will please the reader'.

In fact, it is largely from this book of Gregory's that modern scholars reconstruct what they can present as something like the early *Acta* of St Andrew. Gregory does say a little about Andrew's eastern adventures, about him being sent by the Lord to rescue 'Matheus' from infidels in the land of 'Mermidon', and of his own ill-treatment there, and his conversion of the people. But this is the version of the story acceptable to the Church. 'Miraculous' happenings are few, and the people are not presented as cannibals. Gregory says that Andrew had started his missionary work in Greece, had then gone to Mermidonia, and afterwards to the southern shores of the Black Sea, and so westwards to Byzantium. Incidentally, he does not refer to the consecration of a bishop there.

To continue Gregory's story, Andrew moves from Byzantium to Thrace, to Philippi and Thessalonica. There he is arrested by the Roman governor, the proconsul Virinus, and is exposed to beasts in the arena, but they do him no harm. Next Andrew goes to Achaea (the Roman province of Greece), visiting Corinth and other places but preaching mostly in Patras. There he wins over the proconsul Lesbius to the faith. Later Aegeas comes to Patras as proconsul, and his wife Maximilla and brother Stratocles are converted. It is Aegeas who has Andrew imprisoned, beaten and finally crucified, with Maximilla giving the body burial. In all Andrew's journeyings tales are told of him healing the sick, casting out devils, and restoring the dead to life. In several of the incidents Andrew is represented as stern in matters of sexual failings, and as encouraging the life of chastity.

Gregory does not himself give a detailed account of Andrew's martyrdom; he says that this has been written about by others. It is indeed likely that by Gregory's time the passion story was part of the common Christian tradition, related in the churches on St Andrew's feast day, 30 November (the supposed date of his martyrdom), and referred to in many sermons and hymns.

A later telling of the story of St Andrew is to be found in the so-called *Legenda Aurea*, compiled by Jacobus de Voragine (1230–98), a Dominican friar who became Archbishop of Genoa. This was one of the first books printed by Caxton, in 1483. It was in an English version from the Latin, and described as 'the *golden legende* . . . holden most noble above all other werks'. The book gives a rather slight account of Andrew's life. It covers the Gospel story, and tells very briefly of the rescue of 'Matthew', which it sets, incidentally, in what is called 'Ethiopia', and it includes half a dozen anecdotes of miraculous cures performed by Andrew in his journeyings. It does tell of Andrew's successes in his proselytising work in Patras, and his execution by Aegeas, which the proconsul orders after a long and reasoned argument with the saint, who expounds the meaning of Christ's crucifixion and its necessity for the redemption of man.

The author ends by giving an account of two miracles that were attributed to St Andrew after his death; one is a lengthy tale of a bishop saved, by the intervention of St Andrew, from seduction by the devil disguised as a beautiful woman. This became a favourite subject in the iconography of the saint, and it was depicted in many paintings and in stained glass. The *Golden Legend* was an extremely popular book, spreading widely its eventful stories of the saints, and providing much material for the religious art of the Middle Ages and later.

A cycle of paintings that includes most of the Andrew story as told in the *Golden Legend* is to be found in the Cappella Valeri in Parma Cathedral, Italy. The frescoes date from the early fifteenth century; they are by a local painter of modest talent.

2. St Andrew intervenes to save a bishop from the devil (note the lady's horns). Painting of c.1500 by Bartolommeo di Giovanni (Photo: National Museums Liverpool. Walker Art Gallery)

Such, in outline, is the story of St Andrew's life as it came to be accepted and passed into our tradition. Later on I shall be discussing in more detail how his actual death was described in these sources, but before doing that we have to give some more consideration to the question: how much truth is there in the story itself, in that framework in which the account of the martyrdom was set?

I have said already that I think it is historically plausible to suppose that Andrew went to spread the gospel in Asia Minor and around the Black Sea. I think it is reasonable to make two general points: first, that Christianity *was* spread throughout the Roman Empire, and there must have been people who spread it, and secondly, that once we have accepted Andrew as an apostle and faithful to his commitment to the gospel, then we should expect that he did play an active part in propagating it in some field or other. Why not in Sinope and such places? But whether Andrew went to Greece, and died there, seems to me much more doubtful.

There is no corroborative evidence in the early Church fathers, or in the *Acta* of other apostles. Greece seems to be the missionary field of other men, especially Paul. As we have it, the Andrew story presents a fictitious quality. The names of men who appear in authority in it seem to be of Greek origin, not Roman; they are certainly not those of any Roman governors of Achaea known for the period. Most of the sources have the Roman governor stationed at Patras. Patras, though it was an important city and of Roman 'colonial' status, was not the seat of the Roman governor, who was based at Corinth. The account of Andrew's activities at Patras, and of his imprisonment, and so on, are of what might be called a 'standard' type; it was the sort of tale to be presumed – or made up – as essentially 'true' once there was a belief that an outspoken champion of the faith had been active and martyred at a particular place. It was then further elaborated. The interesting exchanges with Aegeas can be attributed to a serious apologist wanting to put into Andrew's mouth uplifting doctrinal arguments such as might sustain a person facing death for his beliefs. They also certainly reflect ideas under discussion in the writer's own circle and time.

A further consideration must be: what evidence do we have for persecution and execution of Christians in Greece in the period when Andrew, contemporary of Peter and Paul, may be supposed to have died? Certainly when Paul was preaching in Greece there was no active persecution. Indeed we are told of one Roman governor, in office in AD 51–2, who took the line that the activity of Paul was a matter for the local Jewish community, not for him (Acts, 18). It must be admitted, however, that a later governor, or other official, might have been faced with a local situation of rioting or complaint involving Christians, and had people put to death as an exercise of 'normal' policing authority, in a scenario analogous to that involving Christ and Pilate in Jerusalem, but without such tremendous consequences.

Also, it is of course true that in the latter part of the reign of the Emperor Nero there was a seeking-out of Christians, at least in Rome, after the fire of AD 64, for which they were made scapegoats. It is possible that St Peter and St Paul could have been martyred in Rome during this persecution. However it is uncertain, and indeed doubtful, whether it extended far, or in any systematic way, to the provinces.

It is, I suppose, possible that a Roman governor in Greece might have been expected to be more proactive and concerned about the doings of Christians just at this time, and a date of about AD 65 for the martyrdom of St Andrew is reasonable in that we would imagine that he could still have been alive, in late middle age, by that date. We note, however, that Nero had a much-publicised and flamboyant trip to Greece in AD 67 and there is no hint of any trouble with or anxiety about Christians there at that time. We may conclude that, while it is not impossible that our St Andrew was put to death by the Roman authorities at Patras, there is not much of a context in which to set this event, and no positive evidence to support it.

However, there must have been something to anchor the *story* of Andrew's death to Patras, and to provide the son of Constantine the Great, the Emperor Constantius, with the motive to have a search made for the bones of the apostle there; indeed for bones, whether of the apostle or not, to be found at Patras, and to be taken to Constantinople, as they certainly were. I think myself that the most likely possibility is that there was a Christian martyr put to death at Patras, and honoured there at a tomb of some kind, and that this man came to be believed to be the apostle Andrew. Perhaps such a Greek martyr himself had the name Andrew, and this led to the momentous mis-identification. As for the apostle, he may have ended his life in his journeyings in Asia Minor or around the Black Sea.

It may be thought by some of my readers that I am far too cavalierly dismissing this traditional account of St Andrew's life. Some scholars, however, go much further in demolishing it, and a summary of the conclusions of one such academic will show what can be done with the material we have! Professor D.R. MacDonald believes that there is no basis in fact in any of the tales about St Andrew; even the association with 'Scythia' is no more than invention.

MacDonald suggests that the whole story of St Andrew was made up, probably by two known scholars in Alexandria in Egypt towards the end of the second century AD. It was designed to be a Christian counterblast to pagan literature. The authors chose Andrew as their subject entirely on the basis of his name, which happens to mean 'manly', as they wanted to create a Christian hero to set against the heroes that the educated citizenry of the Roman Empire had learnt to honour. In particular, Andrew was to emulate Odysseus, in following a call to travel from Greece to the East, to rescue someone (Helen, at Troy, of course, in Odysseus' case). He was then to have a perilous journey home, overcoming many natural disasters and strange enemies, by the power of the Christian God (rather than with the help of the pagan goddess Athene). Such was to be the new, Christian, 'Odyssey'.

Once Andrew reaches Patras, the model he is designed to emulate, and to transform into a martyr in the Christian sense, becomes Socrates, the noble pagan who accepted an (unde-served) death because Athenian law decreed it. Andrew dies for his, even nobler, Christian principles.

Professor MacDonald says that his authors placed the death of Andrew at Patras in western Greece because this was the nearest to Odysseus' home, the island of Ithaca, where an execution by Roman authorities could plausibly be located. So his theory does at least account for the Patras element in the tradition.

He supports his theory with many passages where the *Acta* of the saint echo or closely resemble passages in Homer and Plato and other Greek writers, and I think it has to be conceded that wherever these *Acta* came from, whoever composed them, it was in a milieu of classical culture – a milieu where Christian apologists were drawing on many sources to get their message across.*

MacDonald does not of course want to incorporate into this early Alexandrian work all of the surviving Andrew material; the wilder and more sensational versions, for example, of adventures in 'Scythia', he accepts would have been later additions to the story. Nevertheless, he is attributing the main outline even of this episode to the original text, and I think he supposes that this had imposed itself on the Christian world, as *the* story of St Andrew, early enough for Origen and Eusebius to have believed (without proper evidence, MacDonald would say) that Scythia was a historical Andrew's mission field.

My own reaction to MacDonald's theory is a sceptical one. I do wonder how such an entirely invented tale came to be accepted as *the* story of the historical personage St Andrew. If – and this is an assumption, of course – Andrew lived at all to be active in the early Church, I would have expected some stories to be told of his actual works and travels. Were these completely lost, to leave the field open to the invention of the Alexandrians? Just as I am prepared to believe that St John lived in Ephesus, and that St Peter and St Paul went to Rome, so I am prepared to believe at least that St Andrew could have travelled around the Black Sea. The trouble is, we still understand so little about the creation and spread of early stories about the apostles, and how one tradition came to prevail over another.

However, that a theory of the kind put forward by MacDonald can be plausibly argued, and taken seriously by reviewers, will I hope go some way to justify my own reluctance to accept any part of the Andrew *Acta* as providing conclusive evidence for what actually happened to our saint. When we come on to looking at how the death of Andrew is described in these sources we have to recognise that we are dealing with tradition and belief. There is no way in which we can reach conclusions about what actually happened. At the most we can talk about possibilities.

## Note

* (p. 16) To remind the reader that these early *Acta*, whatever else they were, were certainly a vehicle for what may be called religious and philosophical propaganda, I refer to another modern interpretation alongside Professor MacDonald's view of the *Acta* of St Andrew, which will bring out its doctrinal impulses. One of the standard works on the *New Testament Apocrypha* (Schneemelcher-Wilson) discusses 'the chief theme' of the *Acta* as being 'the turning away from the world' and 'the realisation of true being in the return to the One, i.e. to God' and suggests that 'Platonism of the middle period' should be regarded as the philosophical movement to which the author was nearest. This interpretation shows how far we have to move from any concept of 'biography' in reading and appreciating the meaning of the *Acta* of St Andrew.

# 2

# *His Death*

In this chapter I quote at length some of the texts that recount St Andrew's martyrdom. I shall not simply give the passages that describe his actual death, but a few that cover some of the events leading up to it. These include accounts of the debate that Andrew has with Aegeas, on the nature and significance of the crucifixion, and Andrew's speech addressing the cross itself. These elements have their own intrinsic interest and artistic merit, and are at least to be taken into account when we come on later to consider why St Andrew was so closely associated with 'the cross', and whether this has any bearing on why he came to be associated with a particular form of 'cross', the X-shaped one.

I start with what we might call the popular texts, which were widely read in the Middle Ages, and which we might suppose to have shaped both thinking and art. These are Gregory of Tours and the *Golden Legend*. Gregory says (chapter 36):

> The blessed apostle was seized by the proconsul Aegeas and put into prison. Everyone came to him there, in order to hear the words of salvation. And he continued, night and day, preaching the word of God. After a few days he was taken out of prison, and severely beaten, and then fastened to a cross. He hung there for three days, preaching all the time of the Lord as Saviour, until on the third day he died, with the people around him in tears, as the story of his passion tells in all its detail. Maximilla took his blessed body, and anointed it and placed it in a tomb, praying all the while to God and asking that the blessed apostle be mindful of her.

Gregory says that he has not written the whole tale of the passion, because 'we know that it has been already told by another, for the profit and the admiration of the reader'.

Jacobus de Voragine made use of a range of material in his account of the end of St Andrew's life (*Golden Legend* sections 90 to 161):

Then blessed Andrew settled in Achaea and filled it with churches and brought its peoples to faith in Christ. He taught the faith to the wife of the proconsul Aegeas and baptised her into new life. When he heard of these things Aegeas came to the city of Patras and ordered the Christians to sacrifice to idols.

Andrew came to meet him, and said, 'You have earned the position of judge among men, and you should acknowledge your judge who is in heaven. You should worship him, and in your worship and penitence give up your false gods.' Aegeas said, 'You are the Andrew who preaches that superstitious belief which the rulers of Rome have ordered to be stamped out.' Andrew replied, 'The rulers of Rome have not yet understood how the son of God has come to show that the idols are demons, and their teaching gives offence to God, so that he turns from them, and does not pay heed to them, and they are themselves captured by the devil, and are kept in delusion until their bare spirits leave their bodies, taking with them nothing but their sins.' Aegeas said, 'These are the foolish things which your Jesus preached, he who was hung upon the punishment stake of the cross.' Andrew answered, 'He chose to accept the agony of the cross, and not for fault of his own, but for our salvation.' Aegeas said, 'How can you say he deliberately chose the cross, when he was betrayed by a disciple, seized by the Jews, and crucified by the soldiers?'

Then Andrew gave five reasons to show that Christ's suffering was voluntary. He foresaw his own passion, and told his disciples it would happen, saying, 'See, we are going up to Jerusalem.' When Peter tried to turn him away from this fate, he was angry and said 'Get behind me, Satan'. He showed that he had the power both of suffering and of rising again, when he said, 'I have the power to lay down my life and to take it up again.' He knew who would betray him, and gave him the bread he had dipped, and did not avoid him. He chose to go to the place where he knew the traitor would come. Andrew said that he had been himself a witness of these things, and he added that the cross was a great mystery. Aegeas replied, 'It cannot be called a mystery; it is a punishment. And indeed, unless you obey me I shall make you experience this mystery yourself.' Andrew said, 'If I were afraid of death on the cross I would not be preaching its glory. I wish you would hear me tell of the mystery of the cross, then perhaps you would accept and believe it, and be saved.'

He began to explain the mystery of the redemption, and to show, by five arguments, how fitting and necessary it was. The first reason was that because the first man brought death into the world through the wood of the tree by his sin, it was fitting that the second man should drive away death by his suffering on the wood. The second reason was that because the sinner had been made from pure clean earth, so the saviour should be born from a pure virgin. The third reason was that because Adam greedily stretched out his hands for the forbidden fruit, so the second Adam should stretch his guiltless hands on the cross. The fourth was that because Adam tasted the sweet fruit that was forbidden, so Christ should taste the bitterness of gall. The fifth was that because Christ was giving to us his immortality it was fitting that he should take our mortality. Unless god had been made mortal man could not become immortal.

Then Aegeas said, 'Go and talk this nonsense to your own people, but obey me and give sacrifice to the all-powerful gods.' Andrew replied, 'I give to almighty God every day the sacrifice of the spotless lamb, which, after it has been eaten by all the people, remains alive and whole'. When Aegeas asked how that could be Andrew said he should become a disciple. Aegeas said, 'I shall torture this knowledge out of you.' And he angrily commanded that Andrew be shut in prison again.

The next morning Aegeas sat on the tribunal and again

invited Andrew to sacrifice to the idols, saying, 'Unless you obey me I shall have you hung on that cross whose praises you sing.' He threatened him with much harsh treatment but Andrew said, 'Think up whatever punishment you want; I shall be the more acceptable to my God the more steadfast I have been in suffering in his name.' Then Aegeas ordered him to be seized and beaten by twenty-one men, and to be tied to the cross by hands and feet, so that hanging there a long time he would suffer the more.

As he was being led to the cross there came a crowd of people, who were saying, 'Innocent blood is being shed for no cause.' But the apostle asked them not to prevent his martyrdom. Then Andrew saw the cross a way off, and he greeted it: 'Hail, cross, given up to the body of Christ, and adorned by his limbs as if by jewels. Before the Lord was lifted on you you were a thing of fear for the world, but now you bring the love of heaven, and are accepted as a thing of blessing. Happy and at ease I come to you, so that you may rejoice and take up one who is the follower of him who hung upon you, one who has always loved you and longed to embrace you. O good cross, you who took honour and beauty from the limbs of the Lord, you have been long hoped for, dearly loved, ceaselessly sought, and now are ready for my eager spirit. Accept me from mankind and give me to my master, so that he may receive me from you, as he redeemed me through you.' After saying this he took off his clothes and gave them to the executioners, and they hung him on the cross as they had been ordered to do.

For two days he hung there alive, preaching to a crowd of twenty thousand people. Then the people threatened Aegeas with death, saying that the holy man, gentle and pious, should not suffer so, and Aegeas came to have him taken down from the cross. When Andrew saw him he said, 'Why have you come here, Aegeas? If you want forgiveness you may have forgiveness, but if you want to release me, know that I will not come down from the cross alive. For already I see my king waiting for me.' And when they tried to untie him they could not touch him because their arms would not move.

Andrew saw that the people wished him to be saved, and

he uttered a prayer from the cross.* After he had made this prayer a brilliant light came from heaven and surrounded him for half-an-hour, so that no one could see him. Just as the light faded he gave his last breath. Maximilla, the wife of Aegeas, took the body of the apostle and gave it proper burial, but Aegeas, before he returned home, was seized by a demon on the street and died in the sight of the people.

It is said that manna as of flour and oil flowed from Andrew's tomb and had the sweetest of smells. It gave an indication to the people of the region concerning the harvest of the coming year. If the flow was poor, so would the harvest be; if abundant the earth would yield well. This was perhaps true in the past. Now, we are told, the body has been taken to Constantinople.

This is the account in the *Golden Legend*. The attentive reader will have noticed that neither here nor in Gregory of Tours' brief reference to Andrew's death is there any indication that the cross on which he died was a special one, different from the cross of Christ's crucifixion. The only detail which *is* different is that in the *Golden Legend* Aegeas is said to have ordered Andrew to be *bound* to the cross (not nailed), 'so as to make his agony last longer.' We shall see that it was a constant feature in the accounts of Andrew's death, and in most depictions of it, that he was tied, not nailed, to his cross.

I quoted above what Gregory of Tours wrote about there being available to his readers a full account of Andrew's death. A task of modern scholarship has been to try to reconstruct this part of the early *Acta* of the saint, using a number of manuscript sources. I shall not go over this material and these arguments in detail, but refer to some passages that are thought to reproduce the *Acta*, and have bearing on the questions we are interested in, relating to St Andrew's 'cross'.

In this reconstructed account, after the replacement of Lesbius by Aegeas, Andrew is represented as forecasting that he will be given up for 'crucifixion' by the proconsul. When Aegeas does order this, he also instructs the executioners not to break Andrew's joints, for he wants him to suffer longer.†

3. Panels from twelfth-century enamel triptych at Trier, showing St Andrew addressing an upright cross and being tied to it by executioners (From: Rohault, *Les Saints de la Messe*)

On Andrew's way to execution Stratocles, Aegeas' brother, who has been converted by the apostle, tries to intervene, but Andrew refuses this. He sees the cross, fixed ready in the ground. Andrew knows this is where he is to die.

He then addresses the cross: 'Rejoice, O cross! Rejoice, truly rejoice! I know that you are now relieved, after so long a time fixed there, weary, and waiting for me. I have come to you, who know of me. And I know of you, your mystery, why you are planted here. So, cross, pure and shining and full of life and of glory, accept me, who is weary from much suffering.' Andrew is then said to have 'gone up onto' the cross, and to have been tied there, by the feet and the top of his arms. He was not nailed, nor were his joints broken, because the proconsul wanted him to suffer, and to be eaten by dogs in the night.

Andrew hung on the cross three days, preaching to the people the while. On the fourth day they begged Aegeas to save him, and Aegeas 'dared to come close to the cross'. Andrew

rejected any offer of rescue, and, 'after again glorifying the
Lord, he gave up his spirit'. Andrew's body was buried by the
wife of the proconsul, and Aegeas killed himself. Stratocles
refused to accept the wealth left by his brother. (See Prieur,
pp. 514–48.)

There are other manuscripts that are thought to reproduce
versions of this basic story, perhaps in some ways less faithfully,
but from these we do get a fuller 'address to the cross' than the
one I quoted above. Here is a part of what Andrew says:

> Rejoice, O cross! Rejoice, truly rejoice! I know that you are
> now relieved after so long a time fixed there, weary and
> waiting for me. I have come to you, knowing that you are
> special for me. I have come to you who have been longing for
> me. I understand the mystery which explains why you are
> planted here. You have been fixed in the world so that you
> may stabilise what is unstable. A part of you is stretched up to
> heaven so that you may point to the meaning of the heavenly
> word. Part of you extends to right and part to left so that you
> may turn away envious and contrary power and may draw
> the world into one. Part of you is fastened in the earth so that
> you may link what is on the earth and beneath the earth with
> what is in heaven. O cross, device which brings salvation
> from the highest! O cross, sign of the victory of Christ over his
> enemies! O cross, grown from the earth and bearing fruit in
> heaven! (See Prieur, pp. 698–9 and 738–40.)

Treatments of the symbolism of the four arms of 'the cross'
can be found in other early Christian writing; there is one in a
letter written by Augustine. The important point to note here is
that whoever wrote this passage was envisaging the cross of St
Andrew as an upright, 'Latin', cross, similar to the one on
which Christ was thought to have died. And this is deliberate
writing; the author is putting plainly what the other sources we
have looked at may have taken for granted, that Andrew died
on such an upright cross. Surely none of them can have had
access to a tradition that placed him on an X-shaped cross? We
shall take up this question again later.

A study of brief references to Andrew's death in the Church fathers, and in Church calendars and so on, confirm this conclusion. As we shall see, there are texts in which Andrew is said to have died 'on an olive tree', or 'on a tree'; otherwise his death is described as 'crucifixion', with no reference to any special form of cross.

There was another relatively early version of Andrew's martyrdom, preserved in Latin and Greek manuscripts, which presents itself as a letter to the faithful, claiming to be an eyewitness account of the events, written by the 'presbyters and deacons of Achaea' (Lipsius–Bonnet, pp.1–37). This has not been thought by scholars to have any particular value, despite what it says about its origin. But this is the story that contributed much to the account in the *Golden Legend*, and the story as believers will have heard it through the ages, at least in the Catholic churches of the West. The *Lectiones*, or Readings, that are prescribed for 30 November, St Andrew's Day, include a brief summary of Andrew's life up to his imprisonment by Aegeas, and a debate with the proconsul, Andrew speaking about Christ's death for the sake of man, and contrasting the pagan idea of sacrifice with the sacrifice of the Lamb in holy communion. This is followed by an account of Andrew's crucifixion, which derives from the 'letter' I have referred to. Here mention is made simply of the 'cross'; it is not described.

Scotland had its own famous breviary, the *Breviarium Aberdonense*, which was printed in 1509–10, on the initiative of the great Bishop William Elphinstone, as part of the concern of the Scottish Church to strengthen a national identity. The work is particularly valuable for information about the traditions associated with the genuinely 'Scottish' saints. For St Andrew, use is made of the whole story of his passion and the events leading up to it, and it is told in the *Lectiones* for St Andrew's Day, and in the readings for the days following 30 November, the 'octave' honouring a major saint.

His actual death on the cross is told of in three *Lectiones* for something that is special to Elphinstone, the *commemoratio* of St Andrew. Each church – in the Catholic practice prescribed by the 'Sarum Use' – had to celebrate three *commemorationes* every week. One was in honour of the Virgin Mary and one in honour of whatever saint the church was dedicated to. The third, in England, was to be in honour of St Thomas of Canterbury. For Scotland, Elphinstone substituted St Andrew for St Thomas. So, the bishop expected the account of Andrew's actual death and reception into heaven to be heard in every church in Scotland every week. (We shall be looking later at Elphinstone's version of the tale of the establishment of the cult of St Andrew in Scotland.)

In this Scottish breviary, the treatment of the story of Andrew's passion is close to that in the *Golden Legend*. Andrew is tied to a cross, but nothing is said about the cross having a special shape. Elphinstone lived at a time when it was believed that St Andrew died on an X-shaped cross, and the saint was shown so placed even on ecclesiastical seals. Yet his story in the Aberdeen breviary was not adapted to take account of this special and distinctive feature of his martyrdom.

I suppose we might expect a liturgical text to be entirely traditional and conservative. More surprising is the fact that nothing is said about Andrew's cross having an X shape in a unique manuscript text in handwriting of a Scottish type of the fifteenth century. This gives a poetic version of stories of the apostles and other saints. The language is 'Lowland Scottish' of about 1400, and the work has been attributed, almost certainly erroneously, to the famous poet John Barbour. The work includes the stories of two Scottish saints, St Ninian and St Machar, but not the story of St Columba. On St Machar the poet comments that he should be better known and honoured in his own land of Scotland. For the account of St Andrew the writer follows the story in the *Golden Legend* very closely, though he adds something from one of the more detailed descriptions of the actual martyrdom. This Scottish poem was composed when St Andrew was well established as the patron saint of Scotland, and when it was generally believed that he died on an X-shaped cross, and yet nothing is said about the special cross. Even more surprisingly, nothing is said about St Andrew requiring special devotion from the Scots.

Let me go back to what we are trying to establish. We have seen that we can hardly claim that the *Acta*, the story of St Andrew's life and death as accepted in the Christian Church, is capable of reliably informing us of what actually happened to the apostle. But that story certainly was accepted and believed, and it is belief that is important. And the way in which St Andrew's martyrdom was recounted in it was bound to affect the way people envisaged his death, and the way artists and craftsmen portrayed it.

So far, however, we have found no written reference to an X-shaped cross in accounts of Andrew's martyrdom. Certainly we have found plenty of references to his death on a *cross*, and only one source which, by introducing a symbolism appropriate to the cross of Christ, definitely requires the belief that Andrew's cross was an upright, 'Latin' one. It may still be objected that his cross could conceivably in fact have been X-shaped. Maybe our sources did not think it necessary to make this plain; perhaps there *was* an understanding that the apostle died on this special cross? Or maybe – whether early tellers of his tale knew it or believed it, or never suspected it – he actually did!

If he did, then such an idea only surfaced, as we shall see, in iconography many centuries later, and explicitly in literature much later still. However, it is worth taking this suggestion a little further, and looking at the possibility that a Roman governor could have had a Christian put to death on an X-shaped cross. In considering briefly the evidence for the way in which the Roman execution by crucifixion was carried out we shall also see how that Roman practice relates to the 'standard' accounts of Andrew's death that we have looked at in this chapter.

## Notes

* (p. 22)   I do not reproduce this prayer; the author of the *Golden Legend* says he has taken it from St Augustine who gives it as St Andrew's in his book *On Penance*. (This, however, is not regarded as a genuine work of St Augustine.) The lengthy prayer asks for release from the burden and the weakness of the body, so that 'it

will no longer hold me back and hamper me, thirsting as I am to come freely to you, the source of never-failing joy'.

† (p. 22)   We note that in these texts there is not the discussion with Aegeas about the 'mystery' of the crucifixion of Christ and the meaning of 'redemption' that we have found made much of in the *Golden Legend*. This element does appear in the readings of the Catholic liturgy derived from the relatively early 'letter of the presbyters and deacons' that I also refer to in the text. It remains uncertain whether there was any such exchange in the original *Acta*.

# 3

## *Execution under Roman Rule*

Crucifixion was one of the forms of capital punishment used by the Romans from the earliest times. It was always within the power of an owner of slaves to have them executed in this way, with good excuse, or with none. Latin authors, such as the playwright Plautus, make frequent reference to the threat and the practice of crucifixion. In the early Republic, citizens could be so executed on the authority of the state, but later on we can say that a Roman citizen was not supposed to be subjected to this lingering torture, though there were notorious cases when this happened. The death itself was regarded as particularly awful and ignominious, compared, for example, with beheading.

Roman cities did not have special execution grounds with permanently erected stakes or crosses (as there were gallows outside many medieval towns), but one significant point about crucifixion was that, whether the punishment was being inflicted by a master of slaves or by the magistrates of the state, it was a very public execution, designed to have strong deterrent effect on the household or on the community. A frequently quoted example from 71 BC is the crucifixion along the Appian Way of 6,000 slaves who had rebelled under Spartacus.

What can we say about the actual process itself? The original and basic meaning of the Latin word 'crux' actually seems to be 'the physical object which was used for a particular form of execution'; we cannot get behind this to a meaning, an idea, with more helpful 'descriptive' significance. Other words that are used in association with, or as a substitute for, the Latin 'crux', and to be understood also as physical objects, are 'furca' and 'patibulum'; these may help us to envisage what crucifixion was originally like. 'Furca' can mean a Y-shaped farm implement or prop; the word 'patibulum' comes from a verb meaning to lie open or be on display, and seems to be used for a large piece of wood used in crucifixion as the 'furca' was. There are passages that suggest that the victim to be crucified had such an implement (or yoke or wooden beam) placed behind his neck with his hands fastened to the ends. Exposed in this way, and, perhaps being forced to walk with this burden to the place of death, he was then hauled upright and (still on the 'furca'?) attached to an upright stake firmly planted in the ground. There are many references to such a pole or stake in the Latin accounts of this final stage in the execution of the victim, and the usual Greek word for the cross is 'stauros', which originally meant wooden 'stake', as used for example in erecting a stockade.

The account of the stages in the crucifixion of Christ in the Gospels can be interpreted as more or less in accord with this description drawn from Roman sources, although of course the Christian tradition has Christ, or Simon, carrying the complete 'cross', on the way to the place of actual execution. In that tradition the cross is pictorially represented as a man-made thing of one upright piece of wood, with another plank fastened across, at the top, or, more usually, part way down this upright.

As far as I know, there is no evidence in Latin literature explicitly saying that crosses came to be manufactured things with an upright and a cross beam, either as carried by their victims, or indeed as erected in this form and waiting for the condemned to be hung upon them. However, I think it likely that by the time of the late Republic there were such instruments (in the style we call the 'Latin' cross) knocked together expressly for crucifixions.

For these executions such a structure was well suited, if we think of the practical and the political effect this form of punishment was meant to achieve: the exposure to a slow death held aloft well in the public eye. We cannot say exactly how closely our Christian tradition, and the 'cross' as Christians have come to imagine and to portray it from very early times, reflects contemporary Roman practice. Yet in one respect I think it is probably right; the main element of the cross was one upright substantial stake, standing firmly in the ground.

We have seen that in the *Acta* of St Andrew the apostle seems to speak of his cross as being similar to that of Christ, and his coming death on it as being a following, even a longed-for emulation, of his master's. In spite of this, people today, who have grown up with the idea that St Andrew died on an X-shaped cross, have claimed that the apostle must have asked to die in a special way, simply because he was unworthy to die as Christ had done. What I think has led to this suggestion is the tradition that St Peter, for this very reason, asked to be crucified upside down. But in the case of St Peter we are told that he died thus in the early *Acta* of the saint, so the story goes back a long way. Also, we do know, from a reference in a writer of Nero's time, Seneca the Younger, that on occasion people were crucified upside down (*Cons. ad Marciam*, 20.3). So, Peter might have suffered in this way, whether at his own request or not.

When we consider whether Andrew could have been put to death on an X-shaped cross, however, we have to conclude that it is extremely unlikely. There is nothing in the *Acta* to suggest it. There is absolutely no evidence that the Romans used such a cross for executions. Even a superficial consideration of the form of such a cross shows how difficult it would have been to erect and to keep stable. The one single stake of an ordinary cross can be driven firmly into the ground, but the two bottom ends of the X cross would have had to be buried deeply, at an angle, to make the thing stand up at all.

It is interesting that few artists who have shown St Andrew addressing his cross, or tied to it, seem to have been bothered by this problem of stability, but one painter, M. Preti, of the seventeenth century, does seem to have been aware of it. In paintings in the Church of Sant'Andrea della Valle, in Rome, he shows Andrew being tied to his X-shaped cross, but this is given extra logs of wood and large boulders, buttressing the two bottom parts resting in or on the ground (plate 1).

There is one practical way in which an X-shaped cross could have been erected, and expected to stay up, and that would have been if it was itself fastened to a solid, firm, upright pole. I mention this now, because we shall have to look later at what appear to be such structures. Indeed, as we shall see, one particular illumination in a manuscript of about AD 1000, seems to show a person on an X-cross that is fixed to an upright. This was thought by many scholars to be a representation of St Andrew, and to show how his cross of crucifixion might have been erected.

This illustration has now been proved not to be of St Andrew at all, but of the Spanish saint St Vincent. Not only that, but the structure to which this saint is tied, if we are to follow the story in St Vincent's *Acta*, is not to be thought of as a 'cross', but rather as a torturing rack of some kind, called a 'horse'. This, along with similar representations in art, will have to be looked at later. I do not think they give any support at all to the idea that an X-shaped cross was used for actual crucifixions by the Romans, or to the possibility that there was any early tradition that Andrew died on such a cross, to set against the tradition of his *Acta*, which we have looked at.

The first classical scholar to write fully about the cross was Justus Lipsius (1547–1606). In his book *De Cruce* of 1592 he writes about the procedures of crucifixion and its practice, both among the Romans and other peoples, and about the symbolism that the cross came to have for Christians. He starts, however, by considering words used in describing crucifixion and the cross, and in the course of this explains that there were several types or shapes of cross. (He tries, as scholars do, to devise a neat scheme, and to fit examples to it.)

He starts with the suggestion that the 'cross' was in some cases a simple upright, one piece of wood, to which the victim was tied or nailed. He then goes on to discuss what he calls 'manufactured' crosses; these are made when two pieces of wood are fitted together. Of these he distinguishes three types: the 'commissa', where the cross piece runs along the top (in a 'T-shape', we would say), the 'immissa', where the cross piece is fixed part way down the upright (as in what we call the 'Latin' cross), and the 'decussata'.

By 'decussata' Lipsius means the X-shaped cross. I think he may have been the first person to use this descriptive name for this cross. The Latin word 'decussatus' comes from 'decussis' which meant 'ten units', or simply 'ten', and this could be used for a coin which was worth 'decem asses'. The Roman silver coin the 'denarius' was, as its name implies, originally such a 'ten-as' piece, although it was later valued at sixteen 'asses'. Since the

Roman *symbol* for ten was X, and this symbol appeared promi-
nently, on coins and in other places, to mean 'ten', a transference
of use developed in the opposite direction. Because an X was used
to mean 'ten', and could be described as 'decussatus', so 'decussatus' came to mean something shaped like a ten, or an 'X', or
something divided up cross-wise or fitted together cross-wise.

In contemporary English 'decussate' is used to describe
structures and procedures in botany and anatomy. The word
is also quite frequently used to describe the cross of St Andrew. I
am avoiding it in this book, preferring the rather clumsy but
easily understandable 'X-shaped'.

In writing about the 'decussata' cross Lipsius describes it as
one in which two straight pieces of wood, of equal length, cross
over each other. He says that the Romans used the word
'decussare' to mean 'make something X-shaped', and he quotes
St Jerome: ' "Decussare" means to divide something by the

4. Roman denarius of *c.*209 BC, showing X
(From: Kent, *Roman Coins*, © Hirmer Verlag, Munich)

middle, as when two straight lines run together and make the
sign of the letter X, which is the form of the cross' (*In Hier.* 31).
Now it is very important to realise that Jerome here is not
thinking of any physical cross of crucifixion, but of the cross as
symbol of Christ and the Church. Lipsius goes on to refer to
other religious texts that use similar language about the X
shape, and these are passages that we shall need to look at later.

Lipsius fills his work with references to ancient texts, but in the case of this X-shaped cross, having written of its use in Christian symbolism, he does not then go on to quote authority for it as an actual form of cross used in crucifixions. All he says is: 'This is the form of cross which today we call the cross of St Andrew, because of a strong and sufficiently old tradition that the saint died on such a cross.'

So, Lipsius seems to have no evidence to offer that the Romans actually used an X-shaped cross, much less any evidence to quote that St Andrew died on one. He claims that the 'tradition' is old; in fact, as we shall see, it is hardly likely to go back more than 400 years or so from his own time.

Lipsius did himself express some doubt about the story. This was not on any grounds that a Roman governor would not have so treated Andrew; that X-shaped crosses were simply not used for crucifixion. It was because there were references to the apostle's death in early Church calendars that simply said he was 'hung on the cross', without giving any information about it having a special shape, and, more seriously, that there was another tradition that gave a quite different account of the death of St Andrew.

So far we have been concerning ourselves with the story of Andrew's life and death as told in the *Acta* and incorporated in the traditions of the Church, at least in the West. To finish this study of what was written about the saint in early times we have to look at the few pieces of evidence that say something different.

The text Lipsius refers to and quotes is from a work attributed to St Hippolytus. This man lived in the third century AD, and even if the work in question is not his, it is likely to be very early. Here we are told that 'Andrew spread the gospel among the Scythians and Thracians, and was then crucified in Patras in Achaea, upright on an olive tree' (Schermann, p. 164).

There are at least two early Greek Church calendars that say Andrew was crucified 'on a tree'; though most of them say simply that he was 'crucified' without saying how (Schermann).

Another text, not given by Lipsius, is, I think, especially telling. It comes in a sermon written by St Peter Chrysologus ( = 'The man of golden words') who was born in AD 380, and was Archbishop of Ravenna about AD 424–9, when it was the capital of the Western Empire. This particular sermon is devoted to praise of St Andrew, who was highly revered in Ravenna, and to the comparison, to the credit of both, of the apostle brothers, Andrew and Peter. Both are to be pardoned for their failings at the time of Christ's death, Peter for his denial of Christ, Andrew, so Chrysologus says (being more specific than the Gospels here), for fleeing the scene. They are to be praised because, having once run away from the cross, they then sought and welcomed it for themselves. 'For Peter ascended the cross [*crux*], and Andrew ascended the tree [*arbor*]. Both strove to share the suffering of Christ, and in themselves displayed the shape and figure of his passion. Both were saved by wood [*lignum*], and rewarded with the palm.' The passage ends: 'So Andrew, our saint, may yield formal precedence, but is equal in labour and in reward'. (*PL* 52, sermon 133)

It may be argued that St Peter Chrysologus is setting out to make, perhaps to invent, distinctions between the brothers here, the more tellingly to emphasise that they were nevertheless of equal merit, but he is plainly concerned to show that 'lignum' can have different meanings, and I cannot believe that he simply made up the story of St Andrew dying on a tree rather than a manufactured cross; he must have had some authority for this in the accounts available to him.

We shall see that the idea that Andrew died on a tree, not a constructed cross, persisted, especially in the East, and that there are even examples of his death being portrayed in this way. Could there be anything in this? Should we rule out altogether the possibility that a recalcitrant Christian thought deserving of death by Roman authorities could have been hung up to die on a convenient tree? Or that worshippers at the shrine of a martyr buried at Patras might have believed so?

I must mention yet another tradition, referred to in the work of Johannes Beleth, a Benedictine monk, who wrote in the mid twelfth century AD. His *Rationale* gave information and instructions about the proper ordering of Church ceremonies and related matters. He writes a little about the life of St Andrew, and his account ends: 'The proconsul Aegeas summoned

Andrew, to get him to sacrifice to the idols. Andrew refused, and as we are told in his *Life*, he was then fastened to the cross, with the people objecting and protesting. For two whole days he hung there on the cross, which many believe was set horizontally [*per transversum*].' (*De Eccl. Off.* ch. 164)

Where this idea can have come from I do not know. We shall see that it too was used as the inspiration for some artists wanting to show St Andrew's death; those who depicted his (Latin-style) cross with one of the short arms driven into the ground, so that the saint's body hung horizontally, not vertically.

I referred in the previous chapter to the numerous early manuscripts that tell of the death of St Andrew. There is just one, dating from the tenth or eleventh century, held in Paris, and known as 'Q', which actually says that Andrew was crucified upside down. This anomaly must derive from 'contamination' with the story of St Peter. It also found its way into art, for example in the Cappella Valeri in Parma Cathedral.

To sum up where the argument has taken us so far: we can say that there is no reliable evidence as to how St Andrew died. In the early centuries of the Church, traditions developed which described his death in different ways. These are ways which might be called at least plausible in so far as a Christian could have been put to death so (in Patras, or elsewhere) by the Roman authorities, and this martyrdom could perhaps be reasonably well understood if the death of Andrew were set in the later years of the Emperor Nero, who ruled AD 54–68.

However, were we to go so far as to accept this account of Andrew's martyrdom, we have to acknowledge that there is nothing at all to support the view that Andrew died on an X-shaped cross, or that, in those early centuries, anyone believed that he did.

# II

*The Cult and Images of St Andrew*

# 4

## *Early Representations*

In writing about the literary evidence for traditions about St Andrew's life and death and cult the researcher is dealing with a limited amount of material, which can be accessed fairly easily – even though at times a second-hand or translated source has to be used. It is true that new discoveries may be made, of manuscripts or papyri, for example, and new interpretations advanced, but most of these will find their way into the discourse of the academic world relatively quickly, and few of them are likely to add anything to make substantial differences to the overall picture.

Trying to give a comprehensive account of the ways in which the saint himself has been represented over the centuries in art rather than literature is much more difficult and challenging. Some of the examples of course occur within manuscript or printed texts, and these are mainly accessible, through books or the internet, if one knows where to look. Many paintings and sculptures are listed, and some are reproduced, in books, usually in works devoted to the history of art; other examples of pictorial representation, in seals, embroidery and stained glass, for instance, have to be sought out in more specialised publications. But how complete and how satisfactory are references such as these?

My own researches, and information coming from local sources, from interested academics, and from observant friends, are adding all the time relevant material, which has never been studied or been brought together to be looked at in the general context. Often such study as has been done is misleading or incomplete, and more personal, on-the-spot, investigation would be desirable. We are dealing here with material in churches all over Europe, and with art and artefacts in museums and libraries all over the world. This and later chapters do no more than recount my own investigations, and such conclusions as I have drawn, and such questions as I have been unable to answer.

There are of course publications and institutions that set out to list material relating to the iconography of the saints, and can provide illustrations of at least some things. I personally, for example, have found the Index of Christian Art at the University of Princeton a valuable and helpful source. Short specialised articles on St Andrew in art are available in the academic literature, and he is naturally given due space in works that cover the iconography of the saints in general, especially in painting. A reference work with very full lists of representations is the *Lexikon der Christlichen Ikonographie*.

However, one trouble is that these treatments or collections themselves depend on earlier publications – they have to be able to give their own references! And I have been disappointed to find how limited their trawls for material can be. For example, the *Lexikon*, published in Germany, has nothing to say about the evidence from Britain, nothing about the seals, embroidery, wall painting and so on, which I shall be discussing later. Also, the listing of evidence taken over from other sources without proper checking can lead to serious errors, as we shall see.

I want to say something in more detail about one particular publication, which I shall have to refer to several times later in this book. This is C. and G. Rohault de Fleury, *Archéologie Chrétienne. Les Saints de la Messe et leur Monuments*, of which volume 10 was published in Paris in 1900. This is the volume that includes treatment of the iconography and the cult of St Andrew. I was able to consult it in the Bodleian Library, Oxford, and a copy is held in the British Library in London.

On each saint in Rohault there is an essay of discussion and there are many pages of drawings: drawings of all sorts of things – such as churches dedicated to the saint, manuscript illustrations, seals and coins, and sculptures. (The work does not include drawings of *paintings*.) Some of the drawings are by the authors; others are taken from earlier publications. Over fifty such pages are devoted to St Andrew. One of the most interesting and praiseworthy things about the book is that the authors do include a lot of British material. There are drawings of Rochester Cathedral, and the ruins at St Andrews, for example, and there are reproductions of British ecclesiastical seals and of Scottish coins which show St Andrew on his X-shaped cross.

5. Page from Rohault, *Les Saints de la Messe*, vol. 10. Note here a statue on Worcester Cathedral, early seals from Britain, and Scottish coins

In this chapter I propose to write about depictions of St Andrew and his martyrdom, other than on an X-shaped cross. Most, but not all, the material comes from the Continent, and most, but not all, dates from before AD 1300. First I shall discuss the way St Andrew himself was represented in the early centuries in the churches of East and West, and in related artefacts, and also the attributes he is given in this art. Then I shall refer to those representations that show him dying on a tree, and to other material that seems at variance with the main literary tradition about his martyrdom, which we have looked at already. Next I shall give the artistic evidence that supports the view that it was generally believed by our neighbours on the Continent – at least until AD 1300 – that he died on an upright, Latin, cross, and that his death should be portrayed in this way. Finally I shall describe the few examples known to me which seem not to fit in with this theory, and write more of what has been claimed to be one particularly early use of the X-shaped cross, an anomaly in the general picture.

The representations of St Andrew surviving from the period down to AD 600 that are best known to us in the West are those in the mosaics of the churches of Ravenna in Italy. There is a lot more material from the eastern Mediterranean world, in the form of mosaics, wall paintings and small artefacts made of metal, stone, ivory or clay. For example a number of small containers ('ampullae') for holy oil, have been found, decorated with figures of Christ and of the apostles. There are two sixth-century manuscripts, from Syria-Palestine, which have interesting illustrations of New Testament scenes.

Two questions may be asked of this material: how can we identify any figure as our particular saint? and in what way are he, and other apostles, being represented? To take the second question first: I have referred above to manuscripts that contain scenes depicting events that are narrated in the Gospels (and in the early chapters of Acts). There are also several scenes from the life of Christ shown in the mosaics, dating from about AD 520, in Sant'Apollinare Nuovo in Ravenna. Some of them, naturally enough, include St Andrew (plate 2).

However most of the examples are not of this narrative type.

Most show Christ with a grouping or procession of apostles; others take the form of a series of medallions with head, or head and shoulder, representations of apostles. Very few of them, it is important to note, show in this early period an apostle in an actual scene of his proselytising work, or allude directly to the circumstances of any martyr's death, though such a depiction does occur, in the fifth-century Tomb of Galla Placidia in Ravenna, where St Laurence is shown with book and cross, with alongside a representation of a flaming gridiron.

It is possible to be sure we have St Andrew in several cases, where the figure or the portrait head is actually named as he. A study of these (Pillinger) has revealed a consistency in portrayal. Andrew is shown with luxuriant, bushy, wild, even spiky, hair. This has led to a confident identification of him in other instances, where he is not named, but where his presence in the biblical scene, or his position, close to Jesus, in the formal grouping of the apostles, would suggest that the figure is meant to be Andrew. In several depictions he is in contrast to St Peter, who is usually shown with a very neat cap of dark or white hair. A good example where we can compare the two is in mosaic medallions on the arch in San Vitale, Ravenna.

It has been suggested that St Andrew was shown with this luxuriant growth of hair to indicate that he was a man of valour. (The story of Samson is just one of many old tales which link physical strength with the hair.) That Andrew should have been regarded as a 'strong' man – a comment made in some old texts – is likely to be due to his very name, which, as we have seen, means 'manly' or 'brave'.

Where a procession or group of apostles was shown, in mosaic or painting, they were sometimes given crowns of martyrdom to carry, but more often they were shown with scrolls or jewelled books, symbolising the gospel they were preaching. It is interesting that early on in his iconography Peter was given a special distinguishing attribute, the keys, those keys that were to open the gates of heaven to the faithful. An example of St Andrew and other apostles being shown with books, and St Peter with a book and a key, is on the seventh-century coffin of St Cuthbert, on display in Durham Cathedral.

In several cases, however, Andrew, unlike other apostles around him, is shown carrying a Greek (equal-armed) cross on a long staff. This has never been interpreted as having anything to do with his own martyrdom; it may signify that Andrew was particularly associated with 'the cross' as the central mystical element in Christian redemption. I shall refer later to some particular examples in Western iconography of this way of distinguishing St Andrew from other apostles (see pp. 142–3).

From these early centuries (pre-AD 750) there seem to be no surviving representations of the actual martyrdom of St Andrew.

We saw that in some early texts it is said that St Andrew died, 'crucified on a tree'; in Hippolytus, 'crucified upright on an olive tree'. (The Greek verb is the one that would also be used for crucifixion on a cross.) The idea of his death tied to an olive tree persists, certainly at Patras, where in the new cathedral there is at least one modern painting showing him hanging on a tree. The other version of his martyrdom, death on a cross, is however also known at Patras, and actually a modern account of St Andrew and of his cult by the archimandrite of Patras combines the two ideas. He writes that the saint was hung on an X-shaped cross, which was designed to represent the letter 'chi', the first letter of Christ's name, and this cross was itself fastened to the olive tree. He manages thus to incorporate a lot in his analysis of the image! Another painting in the church shows this combination of cross and tree.

In 1980 some pieces of wood supposed to come actually from St Andrew's X cross were given to Patras Cathedral by the authorities of the Church of St Victoire in Marseilles (see p. 121–2). The church and the faithful at Patras plainly have no problem now in accommodating these two differing traditions and portraying them. What other, and indeed earlier, iconographical evidence is there for a belief in Greece, or Russia, or elsewhere for that matter, that St Andrew died on a tree?

At this point it is perhaps relevant for me to say that my own very limited research into the iconography of St Andrew in the East, and in particular in the Russian tradition, has not yielded much, for all that the saint is usually said (in the West anyway) to be *the* patron saint of Russia. As figures in early Russian icons, in churches and picture galleries and books, St George and St Nicholas and the native saints are much more frequently found than St Andrew, and I have not myself seen depictions of his martyrdom. I do not therefore have the evidence to say just how widely the crucifixion of Andrew was thought of in the East in early centuries as occurring on a tree; however, I shall write here of three examples of his death being shown in this way, and two of them have Eastern connections.

The Church of St Paul without the Walls in Rome was first built in the fourth century by the Emperor Constantine, and enlarged and embellished by later rulers. In 1070 the church was provided with a magnificent door, of bronze inlaid with silver, which had been made in Constantinople. The church was destroyed by fire in 1823, and the door was badly damaged, but shortly before the fire detailed drawings had been made of it by the artist Seroux d'Agincourt (*Histoire de l'Art*, vol. 4, sculpture section, plates 13 and 16). The door has fifty-four panels, and among them are paired representations of early martyrs, one panel showing the saint as a standing figure in life, the other showing the actual martyrdom. St Andrew is shown being fastened to a forked tree by two men. His legs are together, on or against the trunk of the tree, and his arms are spread wide. It looks as if he is being nailed, not tied, to the tree. An inscription above says in Greek that this is 'Andrew, crucified at Patras'. We have to bear in mind that this door was made in the Greek East, and so it may well reflect local traditions about the saint's death.

My other two examples of St Andrew dying on a tree I came across by chance, and, as I have suggested, there must be others to be found or reported on, especially in churches of the East, of the Orthodox faith. The saint is depicted in a pose rather similar to that on the St Paul's door in a wall painting of the fourteenth century in the Church of Christ Pantocrator at Decani in Kosovo. (I hope this survives!) The illustration shows the (named) saint on what certainly looks like an olive tree, which has flourishing leaves at the top of its divided trunk. His wrists are tied, not nailed. I am indebted to a friend for information about a publication referring to the church and to

6. St Andrew, and his martyrdom on a tree. Part of drawing of eleventh-century door, now destroyed, at San Paolo fuori le Mura, Rome (From: Seroux d'Agincourt, *Histoire de l'Art*, vol. 4)

this painting. The comment is there made that the portrayal of St Andrew is 'unusual' iconographically.

An even more intriguing example of Andrew apparently on a tree is to be found in stained glass in Canterbury Cathedral. The easternmost window of the south quire aisle is a modern composition, placed there about 1960. It incorporates roundels bought from the collection of W.R. Hearst, the American newspaper magnate. These are described in the Cathedral Guide as themselves 'thirteenth century French glass'. In fact I have been told that only a few fragments of the glass are as old as that, and that there has been no recent examination to determine the dating of the roundels as wholes. However, presumably they were purchased by Hearst more or less in the form in which they were later bought by Canterbury, and I suppose they had previously figured, as roundels, in the glass of some medieval French church. I am not greatly concerned about their actual date; what is more interesting is the treatment of the subject matter.

Of the three roundels one shows a saint riding on a white horse, another the saint being seized by two men, and the third the saint tied by the hands apparently to a forked tree – there are certainly leaves sprouting above – and with his legs crossed over in a very awkward fashion (plate 3). The name of Andrew appears in a caption in the first two roundels; the date of these captions is uncertain, but it seems to be accepted by the authorities in Canterbury that it is St Andrew who is represented in this glass.

I have not found any reference to these roundels in the standard sources for the iconography of St Andrew. And I am not aware of any other depiction of St Andrew martyred on a tree in the British material.

We saw in the last chapter that there was also a tradition that the saint died hung horizontally on a cross. There are a few examples of his death being portrayed in this way. Rohault illustrates some drawings in manuscripts, where Andrew is being tied to a Latin cross, but it is one arm of this, not the foot, which is driven into the ground, so the saint is lying parallel to the earth. A fine illuminated initial in a Spanish breviary of the fifteenth century shows the saint horizontally on a cross, being secured by one man above and another below. The ground sweeps up behind, but it looks as if the cross itself is thought of as horizontally fixed (plate 4). An unambiguous depiction is in wall paintings in a church at San Severino, in southern Italy. These are part of a cycle on the life of St Andrew by Salimbeni, and are dated to 1407. The paintings are damaged, but in two of the episodes a horizontal cross, with the saint tied horizontally, can be clearly seen.

The most interesting example of this manner of showing St Andrew's martyrdom is in the Church of San Pedro de la Rua in the old town of Estella, on the pilgrim route to Santiago in Spain. A special reverence for St Andrew at Estella is connected with the story that a bishop from Patras died there on his way as a pilgrim to Santiago in the thirteenth century. It was found that he had with him a reliquary with some relic of St Andrew, which was then acquired by the Church of San Pedro.

Alongside the church are the remaining two sides of a

7. St Andrew preaching, lying horizontally on a cross. Capital of early thirteenth century at San Pedro de la Rua, Estella, Spain (Photo: M.-J. Friedlander)

cloister, dated to 1200–50. Some of the capitals of the columns here are carved with representations of foliage and animals; others have figurative scenes. These include depictions of the childhood and the passion of Christ, and of the martyrdom of St Laurence. Two of the capitals show eleven scenes, one or two on each of the eight faces, from the story of St Andrew. In one scene Andrew is shown seated, preaching to a crowd, in another he is standing, with a man holding him by a rope round his wrist, before Aegeas, sitting in judgement. In three scenes Andrew is shown tied and lying horizontally on a cross. In the best preserved of these fifteen or so people are shown apparently listening to the saint. Among these is a female figure probably meant as Maximilla. Above Andrew is carved the hand of God, showing he is near death. The cross itself seems to be made of roughly hewn branches; if upright it would have had the form of a Latin cross.

The variety of ways in which St Andrew's death could be portrayed is further illustrated in the cycle of frescoes in the Cappella Valeri in Parma Cathedral in Italy. These paintings have been attributed to Bertolino dei Grossi. They date from about 1420, and in one St Andrew is shown tied to a Latin cross, which is placed so that he is crucified head downwards. In churches in Romania there are painted calendars showing the festal days of saints throughout the year, and in at least one case (Humor Monastery) a saint is portrayed in November crucified upside down. This saint is said to be St Andrew (plate 6).

However, these aberrant depictions of the saint's death are not numerous, compared with all the representations from the Middle Ages of his martyrdom on a 'normal' Latin cross.

Rohault reproduces two illustrations from ninth-century manuscripts in the Bibliothèque Nationale in Paris which show the Latin cross. In one of these, the Sacramentary (book of prayers and ceremonies) of Drogon, Andrew is shown twice, first with a crowd approaching the cross set before him, and presumably making his famous 'address to the cross', and then actually fastened to it. A tenth-century manuscript, the Vatican Menology (calendar) has Andrew nailed to a Latin cross, in an open hilly landscape, with a soldier figure on each side. An enamelled triptych from Trier, of the twelfth century, shows Andrew praying to the (Latin) cross, and then hung upon it.

In Catalonia there was a practice of painting wooden frontals of altars in the local churches. Several of these are now in the Museum of Catalan Art in Barcelona. The 'Valltarga' frontal, dated to about 1200, shows several saints, including Andrew (so named) sitting with books, and also a particular scene that has Andrew (named) on a Latin cross, with two seated figures. One seems in authority, and has a raised hand, and above him is written Egeas. This could not be more explicit! A second example, in the Episcopal Museum at Vic, has scenes of Andrew being apprehended and brought before 'Egeas' (named) and then hung on a Latin cross, with a scene of the death of Egeas. The date for this frontal is given as 1130–60 (plate 5).

8. St Andrew addressing the cross, and hung upon it. Illumination in ninth-century Sacramentary of Drogon, MS in Bibl. Nat. de France (Drawing in Rohault, *Les Saints de la Messe*)

Another, rather different, frontal in Barcelona, the 'Tavernoles' altar, of the twelfth century, shows Andrew, Peter, Mary, John and Paul. Peter is carrying keys, and Andrew – but not the other apostles – a long staff topped with a Greek cross.

St Andrew is also shown with a Latin cross in early stained glass windows in some French cathedrals. These examples have been particularly studied by E. Mâle. He found a possible exception at Tours, where he says St Andrew has a 'Latin cross tending towards the X.' I do not think we should take this as significant.

As for sculpture, a particularly interesting example is at the Church of St Andrew in Vercelli, north Italy – the place where the Vercelli Book, of Anglo-Saxon texts, including the *Andreas*, was found. A tympanum over a doorway in this church shows

Andrew being fastened to a Latin cross. On each side are figures on a smaller scale; on the right there is a seated Aegeas, with upraised hand, and on the left a sorrowing Maximilla and two companions. This work dates from about 1220. The sculptor was Antelami.

During the same period, the early thirteenth century, there was an interesting development in the way apostles were portrayed in sculpture on the great doorways of French cathedrals. They begin to be shown, first apparently at Chartres around AD 1200, and then, for example, at Amiens and Rheims, with representations or symbolic versions of their instruments of martyrdom. A commentator on the central doorway of the portal in the south transept of Chartres (Sauerländer) writes that down to 1200 the apostles were figured as assessors in representations of the Last Judgement, but that here they were shown as martyrs, and 'the instruments of their martyrdom may have been introduced to balance the Judge, portrayed with the instruments of the Passion'. In these sculptures St Andrew is given a cross, and it is in all these early examples a Latin one.

A curious representation of St Andrew is in the small church of Besse-en-Chandesse, Auvergne, France. A capital dated to the end of the twelfth century shows Andrew – identifiable from a brief inscription – on an upright cross with ropes tying his arms and legs in such a way as to make the shape of Xs (see fig. 26, p. 136). I shall refer again later to this apparent appearance of the 'X'! It is also appropriate here to mention the sculpture at Auckland St Andrew in Britain, which dates from about AD 800 and which probably represents St Andrew, with ropes forming an X shape tying his body to an upright cross (see fig. 14, p. 81).

In painting, from the time of Giotto onwards, the practice of representing St Andrew on or with a Latin cross continued, as has been shown by the writers on Christian iconography such as Réau and Kaftal. He is so painted by Fra Angelico, Pinturicchio and others. Well into the fifteenth century he could be shown in this way. There is a fine sensitive painting of the saint, with a Latin cross, by Masaccio, dated 1426, and a late fifteenth-century painting of the Florentine school which has him in a busy scene, praying before such a cross. By this time, however, even on the Continent there were many examples of the X-shaped cross used with, or as a symbol of, St Andrew. Its popularity was at least partly due to the institution of the Order of the Golden Fleece by Philip the Good of Burgundy in 1429. St Andrew was the patron saint of this Order, and an X-shaped cross was one of its emblems. Paintings by Domenichino, Preti and Guido Reni, and sculptures such as that by Duquesnoy, still to be seen in St Peter's, Rome (plate 7), all give the saint a cross of X-shape. Gradually the X-shaped cross came to prevail as St Andrew's.

Can we however date its *earliest* appearance on the Continent? Mâle gives the credit to an illustration in a French translation of the *Golden Legend*, dated to 1300–20. It will be remembered that the story of St Andrew in the actual text of this work does not refer to a special shape of cross, but certainly from 1300 or so his martyrdom was shown on an X-shaped cross in illustrations in manuscripts and editions of it. This was the story as it was coming to be believed.

I have myself recently come across a Continental example of St Andrew, not on, but carrying, an X cross which is quite as early. This is a fresco painting on the inside of one of the tombs recently excavated in the chancel of Onze Lieve Vrouwekerk in Bruges. The tomb is apparently datable to 1295. I shall discuss it further in a later chapter (see p. 116).

More remarkable, because of its early date, is a sculptural capital now in the private collection of the Glencairn Museum, Bryn Athyn, Pennsylvania. This was bought in France in 1926. Its provenance is uncertain; stylistic considerations would suggest that it was carved in the Quercy region, Tarn-et-Garonne, in south-west France. The capital is likely to have come, not from a free column, but from an engaged pier in a church, and its date is given as 1100–25.

The sculpture shows a figure on an undoubted X-shaped cross. His wrists are tied with ropes forming X shapes. Each side of him is a figure, looking away, it seems, and each with a hand apparently on the cross (but not in process of tying the victim, or attacking him in any way). It is said that on one side of this

9. Woodcut illustrating fifteenth-century edition of Voragine's *Golden Legend*. The thirteenth-century text does not refer to an X-shaped cross (From: J.B.M. Roze, *La Légende Dorée*)

capital is a crowned and seated man wielding a sceptre, and on the other face is a bowing woman, shown with a halo. Above the figure on the cross is carved the hand of God. This has been interpreted (by e.g. Cahn) as the moment in the story of Andrew's passion, just before his death, when the executioners are ordered by Aegeas to release the saint, and they cannot do it as their arms are frozen (plate 8).

This detail does not appear in those early versions of the passion of St Andrew thought to derive from the original

*Acta*, but it is a feature of the account in the 'letter of presbyters and deacons', which is what lies behind readings in Catholic breviaries, and also behind the story of Andrew's death in the *Golden Legend*. (It is interesting to reflect that Voragine's work cannot in itself have been what inspired the Quercy capital, being written more than a century and a half later.)

I find it very hard to argue with the conclusion that this piece is meant as a representation of St Andrew, with the figures on the side faces to be understood as Aegeas himself and his wife Maximilla. I shall have to bring it into consideration later when putting forward the case for *Britain* being the place where St Andrew's X-shaped cross was 'invented'.

I feel on sure ground, however, in ruling out altogether another alleged appearance of St Andrew on an X-shaped cross, dated even earlier, and so even more anomalous.

Most of the writers on the iconography of St Andrew of the last century, other than Mâle, refer to the 'earliest' appearance of the X-shaped cross as occurring in the troper (liturgical book) of Autun, a manuscript now in the Bibliothèque de l'Arsenal in Paris. This dates from about AD 1000. An illustration in this text shows a figure tied to an X-shaped cross which is itself mounted on an upright pole or plank. Other figures support the lower arms of the cross and assail the victim hanging there with hooks and sticks. I believe the earliest 'modern' reproduction of this image is the drawing of it in the Rohault book of 1900, which I mentioned above. It is there given as a representation of St Andrew and I suspect that everyone has subsequently simply reproduced this attribution without questioning it. So this Rohault depiction is probably the source for the frequently expressed view that the X-shaped cross of St Andrew goes back to AD 1000.

In fact the Rohault understanding of the picture is rather more subtle. I translate the passage of text where the troper of Autun is discussed:

Here we see for the first time the cross fashioned as an X. It has been claimed that this shape only appeared in the

fourteenth century. This page would prove the contrary if
the painter had not added between the branches of the X a
vertical pole. This gives to the instrument of punishment the
appearance of the chi-rho, and no doubt this was deliberate.
The chi-rho, so frequently found in early centuries, had never
been completely lost from Christian monuments, and it is
hard not to see it in this instance.

10. Drawing in Rohault, *Les Saints de la Messe*, of illumination in troper of
Autun, of *c*.1000, MS 1169 in Bibl. de l'Arsenal, Paris. Claimed to show
St Andrew on an X-shaped cross; in fact shows St Vincent on the 'eculeus'
(see also plate 9)

Later Rohault writes:

> The martyrdom of St Andrew is often shown with an X-shaped cross in the thirteenth century. This shape enters decisively into iconographic use, no longer in a rather dubious manner as in the troper of Autun, but as the defining form . . . The British [*Anglais*] seem to have been before us in the open adoption of this type; we find examples of it on Scottish seals, on a painting at Winchester, and in sculptures at Wells and Worcester.

I shall be referring later to this recognition by Rohault of the relevance of the British material to the question of the date of introduction of the X-shaped cross, and also to what Rohault writes about the chi-rho. We shall be asking whether the chi-rho could have had anything to do with the history, the 'invention', of the cross of St Andrew.

When I was first writing about St Andrew in 1993 I was struck by the anomaly: that there should be an illustration of his martyrdom on an X-shaped cross, dating from AD 1000, and then (as I thought before reading of the Quercy capital!) nothing more, on the Continent at least, until about 1300. I wrote to the Bibliothèque de l'Arsenal enquiring whether I could get a photograph of this depiction of St Andrew's martyrdom. I got a short and dismissive letter back, saying that the illustration did not show St Andrew at all; it showed St Vincent of Saragossa. I wrote again, explaining that the belief that it was St Andrew was generally held, and that the mistake was being spread in every treatment of the saint's iconography now being published. In reply I was given bibliographical references and full information. The saint is certainly identified, by another illustration and the accompanying text, as St Vincent. St Andrew is not mentioned or depicted anywhere in this manuscript (plate 9).

So, the troper of Autun does *not* provide an example of St Andrew on an X-shaped cross as early as AD 1000. The earliest evidence for such a cross on the Continent appears to be from the twelfth century.

However, the reader may have been thinking that, even if this particular image is not of St Andrew, does it not suggest that, after all, people could be crucified on an X-shaped cross, and so give some support to the view that St Andrew might in fact have been so martyred? Or does it suggest a way in which an X-shaped cross might at some time have been imported into the story of his martyrdom?

These are interesting questions, and require something of a digression, into the legend of St Vincent and his iconography. This too is a subject with its problems and uncertainties; I hope at least some of my readers will find the digression rewarding!

# 5

## St Vincent and the 'Horse'

It is not surprising that the St Vincent whose depiction we have
been discussing featured in the troper of Autun, because he was
especially revered in that Burgundian town. However he was
not a French but a Spanish martyr. To distinguish him from
other St Vincents, he is usually called St Vincent the Deacon or
St Vincent of Saragossa (Caesaraugusta in Roman times), in
Aragon. It is said that this is the city where he was ordained
deacon by the Bishop Valerius, in the time of the Emperor
Diocletian. He perished in the widespread persecution of the
Christians that began in the last part of Diocletian's reign, from
AD 303.

St Vincent became a popular saint all over Western Europe,
probably partly because of his name, which means 'the con-
quering one'. He is often associated with other 'deacon' saints,
St Stephen and St Laurence. St Laurence is also said to have
been from Aragon in Spain, though his martyrdom took place in
Rome. The instrument of martyrdom with which he is associated
is the grill, and, as we shall see, this is also said to have been used
in the torture of St Vincent. There are in fact similarities in
depictions of these two saints, and the possibility of confusion.

The *Acta* of the saint (under 22 January) claim that Vincent
was seized and taken before a Roman governor named Datianus (not, as far as I know, identifiable from Roman sources) at
Valencia. Datianus orders that he be stretched on what is called
the 'eculeus' as a preliminary to other tortures. Vincent is
beaten and his flesh torn, but the torturers weary before he
does. Datianus says he must be removed for the 'lawful inter-
rogation' ('legitima quaestio') and for worse punishment. Vincent is placed on a grill over a fierce fire, and then thrown into a

wholly dark prison where the floor is covered with broken pottery. Then he is removed, to be revived for further torture, but at this point he dies. His body is exposed for desecration, but it is guarded against birds and a wolf by a large raven. Datianus then has the body thrown into the sea tied to a millstone, but it floats miraculously ashore. It is not said where this was, and there were subsequently disputed claims to possess the tomb and relics of the saint.

Among the sources for this story of St Vincent is a poem by Prudentius, called 'the greatest of the Christian Latin poets'. Prudentius was born in Spain in AD 348, and among his works is a set of poems 'On the martyrs' crowns' (*Peristephanon Liber*), which celebrate the triumph of several who died for the faith. These include St Paul and St Peter – Prudentius has Peter asking to be crucified head down – and St Laurence, St Cyprian and St Agnes. Other subjects are less well known and six of the fourteen poems tell of the deaths of Spanish martyrs.

On St Vincent (*Peristeph.* 5), Prudentius says that Datianus orders that 'he be bound with his arms twisted back, and he be stretched up and down until the jointing of his bones crack. Then strike him with hooks and lay bare his ribs, and see his liver trembling through the open wounds.' The torturers however weary, and Vincent is taken to the bed of coals, and then to the dark prison. There a blinding light appears, and flowers are seen growing from the pottery shards, and angels come to comfort Vincent. He is taken out, and some of his faithful followers attend him. They lick his wounds, and some of them take cloth and 'dip it in the dripping blood, so that they may have at home a holy relic to protect their families in years to come'.*

Prudentius completes the story of Vincent with his death, the exposure of the body and its protection by a raven, the casting of the body into the sea, and its floating to shore. 'That fortunate bay of the lovely coast saved on its sands the holy remains, and granted to them the chance of a tomb.'

What is particularly interesting about this account is that it was written by a man of Spain, and written probably less, possibly considerably less, than a century after the death of St Vincent. Obviously there are parts of the story that we cannot accept. The basic facts of the martyrdom have already been embroidered. However, I see no reason to doubt that there was a deacon named Vincent, and that he was tortured and died for the faith.

The element in the account which we are most concerned with is the extending of the saint on what some versions of his *Acta* describe as an 'eculeus', and his torture there by men wielding 'hooks'. Prudentius does not use the word 'eculeus' in his lines on St Vincent, but in his poem about St Romanus of Antioch he says that the governor Asclepiades 'ordered his body to be hung up on the eculeus and torn, and to be stretched [? – the Latin word here means 'grow'] with hooks and chains'. In this case however the attendants prevent this torture; they warn the governor that Romanus is of distinguished birth, and he orders the removal of the 'hateful stake [*stipes* in Latin] lest he condemn an honourable man to a plebeian punishment'.

Now Prudentius would have known what the 'eculeus' was like; such a structure was probably still on occasion used in his own day. Unfortunately he nowhere describes it. Can we make good this deficiency, and determine what exactly it was? The word 'eculeus' (or 'equuleus') is used in Latin authors to mean a small horse or foal, a decorative model of a horse, or an instrument of torture. It is tempting to assume that this, at least in origin, must have been a structure on which a person was placed astride, though its form may have changed with time.

It is noteworthy – though it perhaps does not help our investigation – that something described as a 'horse' has been a form of punishment in later ages. There was an instrument called the 'cavaletto' in use in north Italy in the seventeenth century, a kind of trestle on which the victim was placed (or actually impaled?), with weights attached to the feet pulling them down. Engravings of old Edinburgh show that there was outside the Guard-house a life-size model of a horse, and a record of 'Public Transactions in Scotland' for the year 1650 describes a punishment for soldiers, known as 'riding the mare'. This might involve, for being drunk, being sat on the horse for two hours, your hands tied behind your back, and muskets tied to your feet, which would stretch your legs – unpleasantly, to say the least.

To return to the 'eculeus' as used in the classical world, Cicero refers once to it as an instrument for the torture of slaves, to get information out of them. The younger Seneca mentions the 'eculeus' as used by the sadistic Emperor Gaius (Caligula), and also, in referring to several types of physical suffering, implies that a person could be *stretched* on it, 'made longer' ('eculeo longior factus'). A Greek word that seems to have been used in contexts where 'eculeus' might have been the Latin is 'trochos'. This literally means 'wheel', and it could be used in the Greek world to describe an instrument of torture to which people were tied.

Other references to the 'eculeus' occur in the fourth-century writer Ammianus Marcellinus. He wrote a Roman history running from AD 68 to 378, of which the books on the later Empire survive. The most explicit description he gives of the instrument is not in a Christian context, but where he is writing of a plot against the Emperor Valens, and the preparations for the torture of a secretary, Theodorus. 'The racks were made tight [? – the Latin is *intenduntur eculei*], the leaden weights were brought, with the cords and the scourges' (Amm, 29.1.23).

As for accounts in the hagiographical literature, these have to be used with care, but they do accord with the impression derived from classical sources that the 'eculeus' was not actually a 'cross', and that it was an instrument of torture, not execution.

There is a St Dorothea who is said to have been martyred in Cappadocia at the beginning of the fourth century. According to her *Acta* (under 6 February) she was placed on a 'catasta' (which means platform or scaffold) and was beaten, and was then taken down and beheaded. A lawyer called Theophilus who had scoffed at her was converted, and was then ordered by the Roman governor to be himself hung upon the 'eculeus'. The *Acta* say that Theophilus rejoiced: 'Now I have truly become a Christian, because I have been hung on the Cross. For the structure of the eculeus has the form of the Cross. I give thanks to you, Christ, because you have allowed me to be raised upon what is your sign.' Theophilus is saying that the 'eculeus' is like a cross (as a symbol of the Church perhaps rather than a cross of execution), not that it is such a cross. The *Acta* go on to describe his torture with hooks and torches, but end with a separate reference to his execution by beheading.

A vivid story is that told in the *Acta* (under 14 May) of a St Pons or Pontius, who was martyred in the third century, and who came from the Hérault region of Languedoc in southern France. He is said to have been 'stretched on an eculeus', but when 'the servants applied their levers and twisted the pulley-weight [*trochlea*] the eculeus suddenly broke with a great crack and vanished in a pile of dust, while the attendants who were there fell lifeless in the crash'. Do we have more useful pointers here as to what the 'eculeus' was like? St Pontius was then subjected to other tortures, including exposure to bears, before he finally died. I write below of early sculptural representations of his martyrdom.

Unfortunately none of these ancient sources actually describes the 'eculeus' so that we can visualise it. It seems quite difficult to reconcile the idea of the victim being beaten or torn with hooks while sitting on a 'horse' (like a gym-horse?), which is what the word itself suggests, with the idea of the stretching of limbs to breaking-point on a rack (as in medieval torture?), which most passages imply. Modern scholars have not been able to get very far with this problem.

There is however one curious treatise, said to have been written in 1573, which is titled *De Equuleo*. I have not found any modern discussion of it and I wonder if we should altogether discount it because of its rather strange alleged origin? But for its very curiosity I refer to it briefly here. The author calls himself Hieronymus Magius Anglariensis, and he says he was captured by the Turks in 1571 when they seized Famagusta in Cyprus and that he was kept in prison by them in Constantinople. He says that he is relieving the tedium and anxiety of his imprisonment by writing this academic study. (Is it a problem that he seems to have classical texts and other works available when he is in custody?)

Magius discusses and rejects some suggested ideas of what the 'eculeus' was like; he seems most to favour a comparison with the 'bench' ('scamnum') of Hippocrates, the Greek doctor, which was obviously some horizontal structure or table on which people were treated or bodies examined. He supposes the 'eculeus' was like it, and would have stood on feet and would have had wheels by which limbs could be stretched. The victim would have lain horizontally, therefore. Magius says that he is adding to his manuscript an illustration of the 'eculeus', as he envisaged it, but this has not survived.

Magius was, it is said, put to death soon after writing the treatise, but the manuscript found its way to the West, to a seventeenth-century Belgian scholar, Sweertius. It is now to be found in a collection of ancient texts, the *Thesaurus* of A.H. Sallengre, published in 1716–19. As I have said, later scholars do not seem to have taken the text very seriously.

Before looking again at the troper and at other iconographic evidence for the martyrdom of St Vincent I should like to stress the particular point that the 'eculeus' in Roman practice, was plainly *not* an instrument of execution. In earlier times it was an instrument for the torture of slaves (and not of citizens). In the late Empire, when citizenship was theoretically universal for all free men, at least those of high status were not to be subjected to it. But it was not meant to end in death, and we deduce from one of the passages quoted above that use of the 'eculeus' would normally precede the formal investigation or trial. I see no reason to doubt that such an instrument of torture could have been used by the Roman authorities involved in persecution of the Christians.

It is not said in any version of the *Acta* of St Andrew that he was tortured on an 'eculeus', but it is said that he was scourged, and such beating is referred to in the accounts of many martyrdoms. We are perhaps justified in thinking that, whereas torture on the 'eculeus' was sometimes used, sometimes not, scourging was always to be expected as the preliminary to crucifixion. The most familiar example of the practice is in the accounts of the trial and death of Jesus in the Gospels. The scourging is not presented as designed to extort information or a confession; it seems simply an automatic part of the condemned man's punishment. In art the scourging is generally shown with Jesus tied to an upright post or pillar, and the beating of later martyrs is similarly depicted.

The scourging of St Andrew is not often represented in his iconography. One example, in the cycle of paintings by F. Pourbus in the Church of St Bavon, Ghent, dated to the sixteenth century, shows Andrew being beaten tied upright to a pillar. However, there are two paintings by Domenichino that give us other scenarios. One of these, of 1609, in the oratory of St Andrew at the Church of San Gregorio Magno in Rome, shows the saint lying flat on a solid table with his feet tied, and a man brandishing a scourge over him. Another painting, of 1622, in the Church of Sant'Andrea della Valle in Rome, has Andrew stretched out horizontally in an X shape with his hands and feet being attached to the tops of four short *upright* posts, with men with scourges to beat him. (It looks most uncomfortable and improbable.) In another part of the painting Domenichino has painted the actual X cross, set up ready for Andrew's crucifixion. I can only suppose that the saint is shown spread out for his scourging in this X shape as another reminder by the painter to us that this was the distinctive form in which, in the seventeenth century, it was believed he died. I do not think the painting can help us at all in trying to imagine how St Andrew would have been scourged. Still less do I think that Domenichino can have been intending here to remind us of the Roman torture instrument the 'eculeus', although, as we are discovering, this did come to be sometimes represented as X shaped.

To get back to the story of St Vincent, we note that, in the troper of Autun, in addition to the picture of the saint being tortured on an X-shaped structure (so often, and mistakenly, regarded as showing the *death* of *St Andrew*), there is a second illustration of his torment, which apparently shows St Vincent on the grill. The two pictures obviously represent just two episodes in the suffering of Vincent, as told in the *Acta* of the saint. His actual death is not shown in the troper. Other iconographic evidence shows his story as a series of episodes.

Dated to 1007, and therefore contemporary with the troper,

are frescoes in the Church of San Vincenzo in Galliano, near Como in Italy. Of the four scenes, the second shows the saint lying on a grill with molten lead being poured on him, the third shows his body being washed up on a beach, and the fourth shows his tomb. The first scene has now been destroyed but a drawing was made of it in 1834. It showed St Vincent being scourged, apparently in an upright position with his arms stretched above his head, as if tied to a single post. In Basel Cathedral there is a panel in relief dating from about 1100 which has a similar cycle showing the saint's tortures and death.

In a thirteenth-century church in Rome, known as the Church of the Tre Fontane, were fresco paintings of St Vincent. They have been destroyed, but were copied by Seroux d'Agincourt (the man who also drew the representation of St Andrew on the door of St Paul's without the Walls which I discussed earlier). There are scenes showing the saint's body being protected by a bird, and being thrown into the sea, and a scene where Vincent is hanging by his arms. These are spread wide, his wrists tied to a pole laid across two uprights. His legs hang straight down. Two men are assailing him with darts (*Histoire de l'Art*, vol. 5, plate 98).

The reader will have noticed that in these cases the structure on which the saint was hung and tortured was not imagined, as it is in the Autun troper, as X-shaped. And I should at this point refer to sculptures that the reader may have seen on display here in Britain, in the Heritage Vaults of Bath Abbey. These are two column capitals found in excavations at Bath which are likely to date from the church building there of 1091. The capitals show two torture scenes, either of two different saints, or of two episodes in one martyr's story. One shows a man with his arms held aloft, both apparently to one side of his head (rather than in a V shape), and being tied thus to some structure by one person, with another raising a scourge against him. The other shows a man lying on a table or rack with two men torturing him with a spear and nails, while an angel hovers overhead. The supporting structure, which is described as a 'rack' in the notes at Bath, is carved in detail, and it stands on wheels, but there is no obvious 'stretching' mechanism visible.

11. The torture of St Vincent. Drawing by Seroux d'Agincourt of thirteenth-
century wall painting in Tre Fontane Church, Rome

(Perhaps it is not a 'rack' at all, but a grill.) It has been
suggested that one or both of these representations are of the
torture of St Vincent, although other possibilities given are
St Bartholomew and St Laurence. If it could be proved that

either capital really was meant to show St Vincent here, then we would have a valuable addition to the early Vincent iconography. But I personally feel, because of the doubts over identification, that we should for the time being leave these figures out of consideration.

We must now go on to look at further examples that do show an X-shaped structure as the instrument of torture of St Vincent. These all come from Spain, and it is perhaps significant that the illustrative material in the troper of Autun, with which we started this investigation, is said to have been influenced by some Catalan model. A Catalan wooden altar frontal painted at the end of the thirteenth century (now in Huesca) shows twelve scenes from the life and the martyrdom of St Vincent. Among these is one showing him being tied by two men onto an X-shaped structure. This stands freely, not on an upright pole. A painting of about 1300 still to be seen in a church at Liesa has a similar image.

12. The martyrdom of St Vincent, on thirteenth-century altar frontal, now in Huesca, Spain (Courtesy of Diputacion Provincial de Huesca)

A fifteenth-century painting, artist unknown, in the Prado Gallery, Madrid, gives four scenes of St Vincent's martyrdom. In the first he is shown on a solid X-shaped cross, which is held firm by small wedges at the base. Two men beat him with scourges while others look on. Next he is shown kneeling on a grill over a fire, with men prodding him and poking the fire, and others watching. The third scene shows the saint's body lying below an elaborate and imposing castle. Dogs circle the body, but are kept off by ravens. The fourth picture has men in a boat throwing the body tied to a round stone into the sea, and also the body, with the stone, cast up on the shore.

All this evidence accords with the story in the *Acta* of St Vincent, and shows that the X-shaped structure in these scenes is not meant to be interpreted as a cross of crucifixion. (It is of interest to remark that, taking the iconography of St Vincent as a whole in Western Europe, the most frequently represented features seem to be, not the torture on the 'eculeus' but the scene of the protection of his body from desecration by beasts, and the millstone which floated him to land.)

There are other Spanish saints whose legends and iconography are similar to those of St Vincent the deacon. In Avila there is a large Romanesque basilica (much visited for its very fine sculptures) that is dedicated to 'San Vicente'. It is uncertain whether this martyr should be identified with St Vincent of Saragossa; their legends are somewhat different. (See *Acta* under 27 October.) The St Vincent of Avila is said to have been interrogated by Datianus, and then to have taken flight with his two sisters, Sabina and Christeta, to Avila. They were pursued, captured, stripped, and in a place outside the town 'they were stretched separately on the eculeus, their joints were pulled apart and they were severely beaten.' They continued to profess their faith, and were afterwards killed somehow with stones on (? – the meaning of the Latin is not at all clear to me) their necks and blows to their heads. Their bodies were cast out, but watched over by a fierce serpent. The legend ends with the novel story of a Jew coming along and being seized by the serpent and held until he promised to bury the bodies and build a church for the martyrs. This he did, after being baptised.

Within the church at Avila is a masterpiece of a sarcophagus dating from 1180. Part of the decoration is a series of ten small sculptured panels showing the legend of St Vincent and his sisters. This includes a scene of the three being stripped of their clothes, and one showing them on X-shaped structures that are mounted on stakes. The device (supposed to be the 'eculeus' presumably) is very like the one shown in the Autun troper (plate 11). The series ends with the Jew being seized by the serpent, and with the building of a church.

In Mérida there is a Basilica of Santa Eulalia. She is one of the Spanish saints of whom Prudentius wrote; he refers to the early church built in her honour at Mérida (*Peristeph.* 3). A St Eulalia is also honoured as the patron of Barcelona and its cathedral. Legends about these female martyrs are similar, and they may have been developed around only one historical figure. The story goes that Eulalia was a young Christian girl (*Acta* under 12 February). She was brought before 'Decianus', and was first hung on the 'eculeus' and tortured, and then (taken down, or still on the 'eculeus'?) attacked with burning torches. The flames were turned back onto the torturers, but Eulalia died, with a dove flying from her mouth up to heaven. Decianus ordered her body to be 'on the' (or 'a') 'cross' ('in cruce'), to be eaten by birds, but a snowfall came and covered the body, and it was later taken and buried by St Felix.

In Barcelona Cathedral there is an alabaster sarcophagus, dated to 1327, holding supposed relics of St Eulalia. This shows scenes of her examination and torture. In one she is shown on an X-shaped cross, mounted on a pole. I think the men assailing her are wielding torches, not scourges, and that the artist here is representing her death, because a dove is shown above her head. There is also a marble choir screen from 1517 with four scenes, of which the last shows the saint on an X-shaped cross (which is not supported on a stake). There is no dove, but I suspect the sculptor intended this to indicate her death. A fifteenth-century Spanish breviary also shows Saint Eulalia on an X-shaped cross. Note that most of this material is rather later than what I have described in connection with the St Vincent representations.

13. Martyrdom of St Eulalia, on choir screen of AD 1517 in the cathedral, Barcelona (Photo: U. Hall)

Here I think we may have an understandable development in iconography. Where legend may have told of torture on the 'eculeus' and of subsequent death by some other means, and where perhaps early representations of martyrdom may have preserved this sequence and distinction, the fact that persons hung on the 'eculeus' could look as if they were being 'crucified', may have led to the belief that it was on this X-shaped structure (as the 'eculeus' had come to be envisaged, at least in Spain) that they actually died.

I have come across similar legends of other Spanish saints, St Felix and St Cristina, and seen fourteenth- and fifteenth-century paintings showing them on X-shaped structures, which the viewer at least might well interpret as meant by the artist as crosses of execution.

My investigations into all this have not been complete; perhaps there are comparable instances in the iconography of other saints in Western Europe. But from the evidence so far, what does it seem we can conclude about the 'eculeus', and how should we interpret the apparent X-shaped crosses in Continental medieval art?

First, there was an instrument of torture, not execution, used in late Roman times, called the 'eculeus', on which it is very likely Christians were tortured. What it was like, in fourth-century practice, whether you were tied upright on it or laid horizontally, these are questions we cannot answer. There is no surviving depiction of the 'eculeus', as it was then, or from the following six or so centuries.

Secondly, in or by the tenth century it became the custom to represent the 'eculeus' as standing upright and the martyr as being tied to it in a V (or Y) or an X shape. Where the structure was X-shaped it was sometimes shown attached to a single stake, which would have given it the stability that it lacks in other representations. The Autun troper of about AD 1000 seems to be the earliest surviving example in art of the X-shaped 'eculeus'.

Thirdly, in most of the early examples the painter seems to be recognising that the saint is being tortured, not dying, on this structure. Scenes of further torments are shown. This fits with the accounts given in the legendary lives of these martyrs.

Fourthly, as time went on the depiction of torture on the 'eculeus' (perhaps especially, or originally, where it was shown as X-shaped) probably came to be interpreted as death by crucifixion. This would have led to the belief that crucifixion on such a cross could have been a Roman practice, if not a common one, and saints who were not by tradition associated with torture on the 'eculeus' were sometimes shown dying in this way.

Another development can be seen in the iconography of St Bartholomew. His martyrdom was written of and shown in various ways. His *Acta*, as developed in the West, included the story that he was flayed while still alive. There is a depiction of this torture being performed in a painting, which dates from about 1300, in Terrasa Museum, Catalonia. The saint is hung like a side of meat, upside down on an X-shaped frame, while men slice the skin off his legs. The structure here is probably not meant as a cross of execution; it resembles the 'eculeus' in several of the illustrations of St Vincent's torture we have looked at – a convenient framework to which to tie the victim to be given ill treatment of one kind or another.

Could this development have had influence on the iconography of St Andrew himself? We have seen that it has been possible in modern times for a representation of St Vincent on an 'eculeus' to be misunderstood as a representation of St Andrew on a cross. A similar mistake seems to have been made in the case of one of the capitals of the eleventh century from the Cluniac monastery of Saint-Pons de Thomières. Five of these capitals survive. Two are in the USA, in the Toledo Museum, Ohio, and these are thought to show episodes in the martyrdom of St Pontius; one of them has the scene of the saint thrown to the bears. Another capital is in Montpellier, in France, and it was for a time interpreted as showing the death of St Andrew on an X-shaped cross (Kingsley Porter, vol. 3, ill. 1269). The 'cross' here has an unusual structure, however, with enlarged spoon-shaped ends to its four extremities, and it appears to be mounted on an upright of similar configuration. The martyr is shown tied by wrists and ankles, and there is a man on each side fastening the ropes – or perhaps, I think, pulling on them. It seems now to be agreed that the saint represented in this capital also is St Pontius. He is shown on the 'eculeus', in a way comparable to the early (Spanish or Spanish-influenced) examples of St Vincent which we have looked at.

Now these misidentifications – seeing a St Andrew where he is not – have occurred recently, at a time when the idea of St Andrew dying on an X-shaped structure has been 'orthodox' for many centuries. It is difficult to see how representations of saints being tortured on an X-shaped 'eculeus' could have given rise in early medieval times on the Continent to the idea that *St Andrew* was actually crucified on a special cross like this, when, as we have seen, there was nothing in the legends associated with him to suggest this, and, let us remember, no mention of the 'eculeus' at all in any version of his martyrdom, and when there were plenty of roughly contemporary cases where sculptors and other artists were showing him on an upright cross.

Another point to bear in mind is that early portrayals of the martyrdom of St Vincent do not show the consistency that might be claimed to support the possibility of imitation. In Spain the X shape for a supposed 'eculeus' – for him as for other saints – seems to be dominant. Elsewhere, as we have seen, Vincent is shown tied to an upright stake to be beaten, or somehow fastened in a V rather than an X shape.

I am more inclined to think that the influence could have been the other way. We have seen that on the Continent there are few examples of St Andrew associated with an X-shaped cross much before 1300. We shall see later that there are such examples from 1150 or so in Britain. I shall be contending that this idea originated in Britain, and from there spread to the Continent. That St Andrew came to be depicted there too as dying on an X-shaped cross may in itself have contributed to the interpretation of other X-shaped structures as crosses of crucifixion rather than as instruments of torture, with the implied, if totally misguided, acceptance of the view that such X-shaped crosses were used for the execution of martyrs in the late Roman Empire.

However, I shall take up again later the (faint) possibility that *in Britain* representations of the torture of St Vincent could have been misinterpreted as depictions of the death of St Andrew.

I hope that this long digression has shown that the troper of Autun gives no support to the view that St Andrew was executed on an X-shaped cross, or that, in early centuries, he was believed to have been. Also, the troper in itself is not an argument for supposing that, around AD 1000, people on the Continent believed that such an X-shaped *structure* was a likely or possible instrument of execution (as distinct perhaps from torture) under Roman imperial rule.

# Note

* (p. 59)   This is an interesting reference to the practice of preser-
  ving blood-stained cloths; these were the next best relics of a martyr
  if you – or your church – could not have any actual bones. Such
  relics were called 'brandea'. This custom has a modern parallel in
  the reverence given to gloves or bandages worn by Padre Pio, and
  thought to be impregnated with blood from the stigmata on his
  hands.

# 6

## *The Cult in England*

Before we consider the evidence from art and artefacts in Britain of the adoption of the X-shaped cross as the instrument of St Andrew's martyrdom, we must look at the circumstances in which the cult of the saint came to England and to Scotland.

There were Christians in England when it was under Roman rule, and many no doubt kept the faith alive even after AD 410. At that date the Romans explicitly abandoned Britain, which was told that it had to look to its own defences against the waves of Germanic invaders. But the firm establishment of Christianity in England has always, and rightly, been associated with the mission of St Augustine, sent in AD 596 from Rome by Pope Gregory the Great.

St Gregory had a particular devotion to St Andrew, and wrote some fine sermons inspired by this saint. Before he became Pope, Gregory had spent some years in Constantinople, and had no doubt worshipped at the Church of the Holy Apostles there. This was a rebuilding of AD 550 by the Emperor Justinian of the church that had held bones claimed to be St Andrew's since these had been brought from Patras in Greece in the fourth century.

Today there is nothing substantial left of the Church of the Holy Apostles in Istanbul, though the old ground plan can be recovered. Ironically it was pillaged by the Crusaders in 1204, and was in ruins when Mehmet II took Constantinople in 1456. In its place was built the Fatih Mosque – the name means the Mosque of the Conqueror – which does survive. It should be noted too that it was in that early sack by the Crusaders that Peter of Capua took what were supposed to be the bones of St Andrew, which he then had enshrined in the new cathedral at Amalfi in Italy. There, whatever they are, they still rest.

There is a story that Gregory was allowed to bring away from Constantinople an 'arm of St Andrew' when he went back to Rome; it seems to me unlikely that he accepted such a 'corporeal relic' as he is on record as opposing the disturbance of a saint's bones. He probably got relics of some kind; perhaps they were pieces of cloth – 'brandea' – taken from the shrine, such as were supposed to be sanctified by contact or proximity with a martyr's remains.

In Rome Gregory had already been responsible for the foundation of a monastery in honour of St Andrew, which occupied the site of the palatial home on the Caelian Hill that Gregory had inherited from his rich family. Gregory may himself have been abbot there for a while, and the Augustine he sent to England had been prior of this monastery.

In AD 597 Augustine arrived in Kent, where the wife of King Ethelbert was a Frankish princess who was a Christian. In Canterbury there was an old church dating from the time of Roman occupation, dedicated to St Martin of Tours, and this became Augustine's first base. He then went on to found a church which he dedicated to the Saviour, which became Canterbury Cathedral, and a monastery of St Peter and St Paul, later known as St Augustine's.

With two other foundations Augustine recalled the mission's link with the monastery on the Caelian Hill in Rome. He founded a church in Canterbury to St Pancras, a boy martyr whose family had once owned land on that Roman site, and the first church built and dedicated outside Canterbury was founded in the name of St Andrew. This was at Rochester, which became the centre of the see of the second bishop to be created in this establishment or re-establishment of structures of the Christian Church in England. Rochester Cathedral is in fact no longer dedicated in St Andrew's name, but in the name of Christ and the Blessed Virgin Mary. The cathedral building now displays no significant representations of St Andrew, but I shall later be describing important church seals of Rochester which do depict the saint (see pp. 102–3).

St Andrew became a popular saint in Anglo-Saxon England, and several churches were dedicated to him in the seventh and eighth centuries. There is an interesting example, which still retains some of its Saxon wooden wall-timbers, at Greensted in Essex.

From the fact that it is listed in early Church calendars we know that in Saxon times the feast of St Andrew was celebrated on 30 November, and there is a ninth-century martyrology in Old English which refers to Andrew's preaching in Scythia and Achaea, and briefly recounts his death. Together with writings on other apostles there are preserved homilies or sermons, and poems for religious use, on the subject of St Andrew, attributed to well-known churchmen including Aelfric, Alcuin and Bede.

Among the thirteen Latin hymns attributed to Bede there are two in honour of St Andrew. One describes his call by Christ, and refers to his preaching among the Greeks and to his fortitude in death. The other gives a poetic version of Andrew's address to the cross and words welcoming martyrdom. I give a translation of some lines, which, incidentally, will show that the poet was not thinking of St Andrew being put to death on a cross of special shape.

> Hail, memorial of glory,
> Hail, holy mark of victory,
> By which God in death
> Saved our lost world.
> O Cross, you shine forth,
> Splendid in glittering virtue,
> And Christ himself made you holy
> With the limbs of his own body.
> [. . .]
> Now I rejoice that I come to you,
> I embrace you with the arms of love,
> And with your help I climb to heavenly joys.
> [. . .]
> So spoke Andrew when he saw
> Standing there the arms of the cross;
> He gave his clothing to the soldiers,
> And was raised on the tree that gives life.

Note the word 'tree'. The poet certainly uses the Latin 'arbor', but here he does not mean it in the literal sense (as we saw St Peter Chrysologus did in comparing the deaths of Peter and Andrew) (see p. 35). From early times 'arbor' or 'tree' *could* be used for the cross of crucifixion. As for 'the arms of the cross', the word used is 'cornua'. The basic meaning of 'cornu' is 'horn', but the word has many derived uses in Latin. 'Cornua' can be, for example, the 'wings' of an army, or the 'yard-arms' of a sailing-ship. Here surely the poet is thinking of the spreading arms of a 'Latin' cross. For it is plain from the whole passage that he imagines Andrew speaking to, and dying upon, a cross that is the same as the cross on which Christ died.

All this seems to derive in essence from the standard, ortho-dox, view of the saint's mission and martyrdom. We have seen that a more dramatic and colourful story, with adventures among cannibals, was known in England, and was preserved in the *Andreas*, though this actual poetic text was composed probably a century, even two, after the time of Bede. It is interesting to reflect on the differing ideas about the character and significance of St Andrew that may have been current and of appeal in Anglo-Saxon England.

We have seen how St Augustine came to Kent in AD 597, and that this led to the reintroduction or consolidation of Chris-tianity in the south of England. But by that time there had also been a remarkable movement of Christian missionaries of a different type in what we now think of as Scotland.

In fact, there is evidence for the work of a 'Roman' style Bishop Ninian based at Whithorn in Galloway, around AD 400. Bede, in his *Ecclesiastical History*, says that Ninian brought faith to 'the southern Picts', but it is controversial where and how far Ninian travelled; how much of southern and eastern Scotland was converted by him. In any case, what was more important for the religious history of Scotland was the coming from Ireland of groups of proselytising monks, starting with the arrival on the island of Iona, off Mull, in AD 563, of the energetic and charismatic holy man, St Columba. Columba and his followers certainly took the faith all over southern and eastern Scotland, up to Inverness and beyond. They established their simple monastic communities in many places, often on rather remote sites by the sea, and they secured the adherence of the kings, the 'Picts' in the east and the 'Scots' in the west.

This 'Celtic' Christianity was very different, not so much in doctrine (though there were points of variance) as in organisation and lifestyle, from the 'Roman' Christianity brought by St Augustine's mission to Kent. (I use inverted commas here and elsewhere, in recognition of the fact that modern scholarship has reacted against what is seen as an overemphasis on differences in the two traditions, and a degree of romanticisation of things Celtic.) This mission, as we have seen, had been accomplished through the initiative of the Pope. The strong link with Rome continued, and influenced the practices and the organisation of the Church as its power and appeal spread. A great advance seemed to have been made in AD 627 when Bishop Paulinus secured the conversion of King Edwin of Northumbria. He was baptised at York, which was planned to be the second metropolitan see, after Canterbury, for the whole of Britain. However, Edwin was killed in AD 632, fighting against the still pagan kings, Penda of Mercia and the Welsh Cadwallon.

This defeat was soon reversed by the victory at Heavenfield near Hexham in AD 633 of a prince of a different Northumbrian line, Oswald. He established himself as king of Northumbria, and overlord of much of England. Now Oswald had spent time in exile in Iona, and once established he looked north, not to Canterbury, for the model to rebuild Christianity in his kingdom. The missionary Aidan was brought from Iona, and consecrated bishop. Aidan rejected the idea of basing himself at York, and chose instead Lindisfarne, off the Northumbrian coast, a place similar to Iona.

Sooner or later the two forms of Christian life and worship would collide and struggle to prevail. In fact it was in the reign of Oswald's successor, Oswiu, that disputes over the date of Easter and other matters led to the king convening a meeting, virtually to decide between the 'Celtic' Church and Rome. This was the Synod of Whitby, held in AD 664. What seems to have been the decisive argument for the king was that the authority of St Peter, who was 'the rock' on which the Church was founded and the 'holder of the keys' of heaven, must prevail over St Columba. The result was the departure of Bishop Colman and his followers from Lindisfarne, and the triumph of the 'English' Church, with its aspirations to rule over the whole of Britain, and with its centre in the north at York, with its church there dedicated to St Peter.

I have gone into some detail over these developments because we shall need to consider later the religious attitude and policies of Pictish kings, and because the chief spokesman and champion of the 'Roman' side at the Synod of Whitby was the powerful ecclesiastic, Wilfrid, who fostered the cult of St Andrew in northern England.

Wilfrid was born in AD 634 at Ripon, and was educated at Lindisfarne, but he went to Rome, and a stay there and at Lyon convinced him of the need to adopt Roman doctrine and Roman ways. He was actually consecrated a bishop at Lyon in AD 664, ready to exercise authority once the decision had been made against the 'Celtic' Church, as it was, largely indeed by his own advocacy, at the Synod of Whitby. Wilfrid went on to have a chequered career as churchman and missionary, until his death in AD 709 at a monastery 'of St Andrew' which he had founded at Oundle.

Wilfrid's biographer says that he particularly honoured St Peter and St Andrew, and brought relics of these saints to Britain from Rome. In addition to several monasteries he founded a great church at Ripon, dedicated to St Peter, and one at Hexham, dedicated to St Andrew. Many believe that this church played a part in the establishment of the cult of St Andrew in Scotland, and that relics of the saint may have come from Hexham to St Andrews.

I have referred already to the *Ecclesiastical History of the English People*, written by Bede as a monk at Jarrow. His account goes down to AD 731; Bede himself died four years later. The book is by far the most important single source for that spread of Christianity in England which I have been summarising, and which had triumphed among the Anglo-Saxons by AD 731. We shall see that Bede's work also contains significant references to developments in Scotland.

Before I write in more detail about these it is appropriate to raise a question that may occur to the reader – with this interest in St Andrew in England what portrayals of the saint survive there from Anglo-Saxon times? I wrote in an earlier chapter of the coffin of St Cuthbert, who died in AD 687. This is now in Durham Cathedral. On it there are formalised half-length representations of several apostles. One is named as 'Andreas'; he carries a book. Next to him is 'Petrus', carrying a book and a large key. The only other particular 'St Andrew' I know of is on the shaft of a stone cross at Auckland St Andrew, near Durham, dating to about AD 800. This shows a figure bound to what appears to be a 'Latin' cross, and most scholars accept that it is meant to be St Andrew. I shall discuss this later (see pp. 137–9). What I find of special interest is that, as far as I know, this may be the *only* representation of St Andrew dying on a Latin cross made in Britain, in any period, from the sixth century until today. So completely has the X-shaped cross come to dominate the saint's iconography here!

14. Part of cross of AD 800 at Auckland St Andrew, Tyne and Wear (Photo: T. Middlemass. © Corpus of Anglo-Saxon Stone Sculpture, University of Durham)

# 7

## *The Cult in Scotland*

We have seen that Columba and other missionaries in the 'Celtic' tradition travelled widely in Scotland, and there is plenty of evidence of their activity and their success in the east, in those parts which in the sixth and subsequent centuries were under Pictish kings. Fife, where the town of St Andrews was to be founded on the headland of Kinrymont, was certainly a part of Pictland. We know of a companion of Columba, Cainnech, who, some have thought, could have given his name to the town of Kennoway in Fife. In eleventh-century notes to an early Irish martyrology this man is said to have gone to 'Cill Rig-monaidh' in 'Alba' (which is the Gaelic name for Scotland). This suggests the possibility that he, or perhaps another follower of Columba, established a community of monks at 'Kinrymont' (later known as 'Kilrymont'). This would have been in the late sixth century. The discovery of early Christian graves at two places in the area fits in with the supposition that there was Christian worship here long before there is any likelihood of the site being dedicated to St Andrew – that St Andrew who was of course to give the place its historic name.

In the seventh century Pictish kings were under pressure from the expanding and confident power of the Anglian rulers of Northumbria. In the time of Oswald and his successors the lands south of the Forth were under their control, and this control involved also the attempt to impose the authority of the 'English' Church in the Lothians and beyond, among the Picts. Bede tells us of Archbishop Theodore consecrating at York a bishop, Trumwine, 'to be bishop of those Picts who were then subject to English rule'. Trumwine was based at a monastery in Abercorn, in West Lothian.

His consecration took place in the reign of Oswiu's son, the ambitious King Ecgfrith, who ruled from AD 670 to 685. Early in his reign Ecgfrith defeated a force led south by the Pictish King Brudei, and in AD 685 he decided – against advice, Bede says – to go north and ravage Pictland. He was lured into narrow passes by the Picts, and totally defeated. The king was killed, and we are told that many English had to flee south, including Bishop Trumwine. This victory over Ecgfrith at Dunnichen Moss (or 'Nechtansmere'), near Forfar in Angus, is mentioned in a number of other sources, and the battle may be commemorated in a scene on a Pictish carved stone in Aberlemno churchyard.

The Picts were thus freed for the time from the political and the religious empire-building from the south. However, their engagement with their southern neighbours, and no doubt a growing awareness of the world and sophistication in their own culture brought a greater susceptibility, especially among their rulers and churchmen, to outside influences. This had momentous consequences in the reign of a certain Nechtan, in the early eighth century.

Bede tells us that, about AD 710, Nechtan, king of the Picts, after studying Church writings, and believing that his priests were wrongly calculating the date for the celebration of Easter, wrote to Abbot Ceolfrith at the monastery of Wearmouth and Jarrow, asking for guidance on this and other points, and asking also for architects to come and build him a stone church in the Roman style. He said he would dedicate this in the name of St Peter. Bede gives a very long reply on the doctrinal matters, quoting various scriptural authorities, and also on the Church's method of calculating the date of Easter each year; it is likely, at least possible, he wrote this himself, for Ceolfrith to send.

This letter (in Latin, of course) was read to King Nechtan and his learned men, and translated 'into their own tongue', and the king 'fell to his knees, thanking God that he had been thought worthy to receive such a gift from the land of the Angles'. He at once adopted the Roman practice of calculating Easter on a nineteen-year cycle, and also the Roman form of tonsure for priests, and, Bede says, 'the people, freed from error, rejoiced that they were now under the direction of Peter, the most blessed chief of the Apostles, and were safe in his protection'.

Nechtan must have been responsible for a complete change in religious direction; Irish annals for the year AD 717 record 'the expulsion of the community of Iona across the ridge of Britain by King Nechtan'. This reminds us of Colman and his monks leaving Lindisfarne after the Synod of Whitby. We presume that Nechtan got his stone church dedicated to St Peter. (It has been suggested that it was at Restenneth in Angus.) Such a church represented a new kind of cult, and perhaps an elaboration of worship, compared with simpler practices in the Iona tradition.

Nechtan entered a monastery in AD 724, and there seem to have been some years of struggle between rivals for power, but from about AD 730 to 761 the Picts were ruled by a strong and successful king, Angus (to give the convenient English form of his name).* Many believe that it was under this king that the cult of St Andrew was introduced to Pictland, and a church in his name built at Kinrymont in Fife. As we shall see the institution of such a cult is credited in legend to a 'King Hungus', and one Chronicle says that relics of St Andrew came to Scotland in AD 761. It seems historically plausible that a king of this date should have followed the precedent of Nechtan, and have set up for the Picts the cult of another of the highly revered apostles, Peter's brother Andrew. In doing this he will have taken over and transformed the 'Celtic' religious site which we have seen is likely to have already existed at Kinrymont.

It may be that an additional incentive to institute the cult came from Hexham, the Church of St Andrew founded in Northumbria by St Wilfrid. After the death of Wilfrid in AD 709 a certain Acca became bishop at Hexham, and we are told that he too collected relics and had a special reverence for St Andrew. A chronicler reports that Acca was for some reason expelled from his see in 732, and it has been suggested that he might have taken refuge with the Picts in Fife. Perhaps he helped King Angus in the foundation of the cult of St Andrew,

1. The martyrdom of St Andrew. Painting by M. Preti in Sant'Andrea della Valle, Rome, 1650–1 (The Bridgeman Art Library)

2. The call of Peter and Andrew. Sixth-century mosaic in Sant'Apollinare Nuovo, Ravenna (The Bridgeman Art Library, London)

4. St Andrew lying horizontally on cross. Illumination in fifteenth-century Breviary of Martin of Aragon (MS Roth. 2529. Bibliothèque Nationale de France)

3. St Andrew martyred on a tree. Roundel from window s. xiv, Canterbury Cathedral (Photo: M. Tucker. By kind permission of the Dean and Chapter, Canterbury)

5. Martyrdom of St Andrew, on twelfth-century altar frontal from Sant Andreu de Sagas, now in Vic Museum, Spain (Photo: G. Salvans. MEV 1615, Museu Episcopal de Vic)

7. Nineteenth-century statue of St Andrew, formerly on North British Mercantile and Insurance Company building in Edinburgh, now at Botanic Garden, St Andrews. Based on Duquesnoy statue of St Andrew in St Peter's, Rome (Photo: U. Hall)

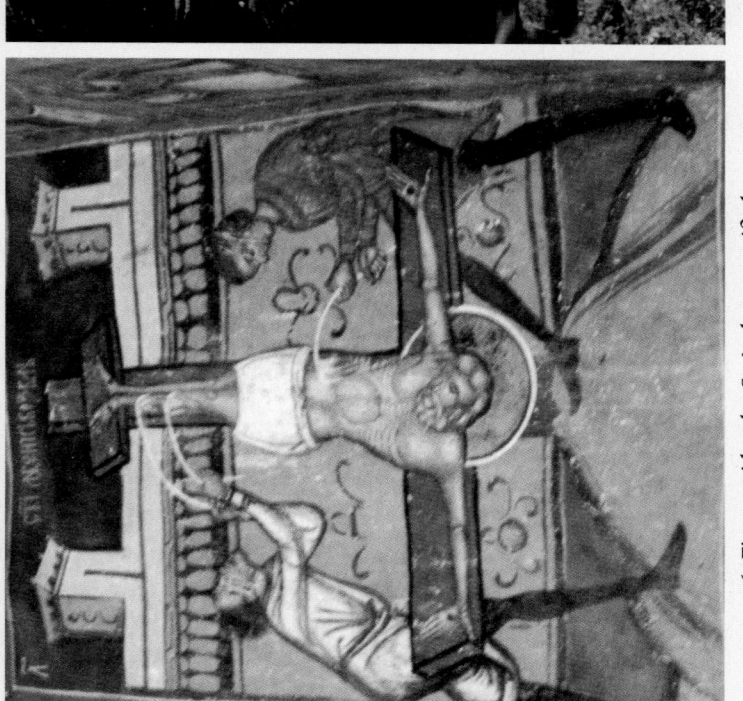

6. Figure said to be St Andrew, crucified upside down. Humor Monastery, Romania (Photo: C. Gascoigne)

8. The earliest representation known to date of St Andrew on an X-shaped cross? Capital dated to AD 1100–25 from Quercy region, France. Now in Glencairn Museum, Bryn Athyn, PA, USA (Photo: courtesy of Glencairn Museum, Academy of the New Church)

9. Illumination from Troper of Autun, showing St Vincent on the 'eculeus'
(MS 1169, Bibl. de l'Arsenal, Paris. Courtesy of Bibliothèque Nationale de France)

10. Tomb painting of late thirteenth century. Church of Our Lady, Bruges, Belgium. (Photo: courtesy of Welcome Church of Our Lady, Bruges)

11. Scenes of martyrdom of St Vincent of Avila and his sisters, on sarcophagus of AD 1180 in Church of San Vicente, Avila, Spain (Photo: M.-J. Friedlander)

12. Thirteenth-century pilgrim badge (33 x 27mm), found at Perth (Courtesy of Perth Museum and Art Gallery, Perth and Kinross Council, Scotland)

13. Page from Huntingfield Psalter showing martyrdoms of St Peter, St Paul, St Andrew, St James. (© The Pierpont Morgan Library, New York MS M. 43, f. 25)

ABOVE.

14. Macclesfield Psalter (Fitzwilliam Museum, Cambridge)

OPPOSITE.

15. Figure of St Andrew in the Mauley window (s32) in York Minster (Photo: N. Teed.
Reproduced by kind permission of the Dean and Chapter of York)

16. Twelfth-century wall painting of St Andrew (?) in Church of
St Mary Magdalene, Ickleton, Cambs (Photo: M. Wallace)

17. The 'Cottam font', dated to *c.*1140, in Langtoft Church, Driffield, Yorks.
(Photo: M. Chandler)

18. Reliquary of St Andrew's sandal, *c.*1000, in Trier
(From: Lasko, *Ars Sacra*, © Hirmer Verlag, Munich)

19. Shield with chi-rho, mosaic of 547 in San Vitale, Ravenna
(The Bridgeman Art Library, London)

20. Wall painting from Seu d'Urgell, now in Museum of Catalan Art, Barcelona, showing St Peter and St Andrew with attributes (Photo: Calveras, Mérida, Sagrista. © MNAC – Museu Nacional d'Art de Catalunya, Barcelona, 2005)

and relics of the saint were brought by him. Or possibly they came later from Hexham, because of a continuing link between the two places. Acca died in AD 740; where this was we do not know, but I believe his body was taken back to Hexham and given honourable burial there.

It is worth recalling that Bede's *History* does not extend beyond AD 731. It ends therefore before the expulsion of Acca from Hexham, and cannot contribute to the elucidation of that episode. And Bede, having written in some detail about Nechtan and the cult of St Peter, says nothing about the institution of a cult of St Andrew in Scotland. I think we can be sure that such a cult had not been set up by AD 731.

As we shall see the legends about the origin of the cult of St Andrew at Kinrymont do not say anything about influence from the south, from Northumbria, from Hexham. In later generations the establishment of Church and State in Scotland would have wanted to play down, or indeed to ignore or eliminate, any evidence that the Scottish Church, with its bishop at St Andrews, owed something to the Church in Northumbria, in England, and should be expected to accept the authority of the Archbishop of York.

It is possible, then, that in the mid eighth century the Pictish king Angus, with or without help from Acca or Hexham, but surely influenced, as Nechtan had been, by contacts with the English Church, instituted the cult of St Andrew, and had the first church built in his honour in Scotland. A reference in the Annals of Ulster for AD 747 to the death of Tuathalan, who is described as 'abbot at Cennrigmonaid', is certain evidence for some important religious foundation at Kinrymont in the eighth century.

Another, less attractive, possibility is that the cult was instituted a century later, by a second 'King Angus', who ruled from AD 820 to 834. He is credited with the foundation of 'Kilrimund' in some sources.

I do not think it is necessary to discuss further the arguments for and against these different theories. We can accept that a Pictish king in the eighth or ninth century AD founded a church in the name of the apostle Andrew at Kinrymont in Fife. There is evidence from the following centuries of the existence and the growing importance of this religious foundation, and the saint's shrine was attracting many pilgrims by the time of King Malcolm III of Scotland and his wife Queen (later 'Saint') Margaret (d.1093). It was she who instituted the ferry across from Lothian to Fife for the use of pilgrims, at 'Queensferry'. One version of the foundation legend of St Andrews which I refer to in the next chapter, which dates from 1100 or so, gives a catalogue and description of these pilgrims, as coming even then from many Continental lands. Two in particular of the sons of Queen Margaret, Alexander I (d.1124) and David I (d.1153), brought further vitality to the church in St Andrews with grants of land and the creation there of a community of Augustinian canons.

Next we do need to look at this legend, the stories which developed around the historical fact of the establishment of the cult of the saint, and to see if they have any bearing on the problem of the connection of the X-shaped cross with St Andrew.

First however we should take up the question raised in connection with the cult in England, and consider whether there is any surviving representation of St Andrew dating from these early centuries in Scotland.

A Pictish stone found recently in the excavations at Tarbat, Portmahomack, Easter Ross, and dated to about AD 800, formed part of a large cross slab. The surviving top corner shows on one side part of the carving of the cross and a 'dragon' (hence the name 'the dragon stone'), and on the other side part of a frieze of animals, including lions, and below this a row of clerical personages. Parts of four of these survive, and it is suggested that across the whole face of the stone there could have been a row of apostle figures, perhaps with Christ. Representations of apostles appear in the carving of Northumbrian crosses of this period, and the Pictish work at Tarbat is said to show some Northumbrian influence.

It is interesting that the figures on this stone are carved with great individuality in face, hair and dress. One carries a book, the next has particularly bushy, spiky hair. He carries *something*

15. Drawing of figures on Pictish stone, TR20,
in Tarbat Discovery Centre, Portmahomack, Ross
(Drawing: G. Scott. Reproduced by permission of
Tarbat Discovery Centre)

– not a book (it looks like a fish to me!). Of the other two, less survives and we cannot judge of their attributes. It has been suggested that the figure with the wild hair may be meant to be St Andrew. We saw earlier that there are several early representations of the saint, in paintings and mosaics, which show Andrew in this way, and that this feature may be due to the connotation of the name Andrew. It is indeed tempting to identify the figure on the Tarbat stone as the saint, and of course a depiction of him and the other apostles around AD 800 would fit in well enough with cults of St Peter and St Andrew being established by the Picts in the period of King Nechtan and his successors.

I may add to this evidence the fact that another fragment from Tarbat, found a hundred years ago, and now in Edinburgh, is thought to be part of the same cross. It has a Latin inscription on the narrow side of the stone, which says 'In the name of Jesus Christ, the cross of Christ' ('CRUX XRI') 'in memory of Reo . . .' We note the use of Latin here. Note too the phrase 'the cross of Christ'; we shall come across this again in versions of the legend concerning the foundation of St Andrews, discussed in the next chapter.

A considerably later stone, now at Dunkeld Cathedral, has three panels, a scene with a crowd of heads, and below it two rows of six figures each, not much differentiated. These are thought to be the twelve apostles; indeed the stone is popularly known as 'the apostle stone'.

## Note

* (p. 84)   The sequence and relationship between the recorded Pictish kings are matters of controversy. Doubt has been thrown on the common contention that the succession was matrilinear. Other problems are whether certain kings are to be thought of as merely local rulers, or as Pictish 'high-kings', and what links there were with other royal families in Scotland. Fortunately we do not need to tackle these questions!

# 8

# *The Foundation Legend of St Andrews*

We have seen that there is a popular belief that St Andrew was put to death on an X-shaped cross, but that there is nothing in the early stories about the saint to account for or to justify this tradition. In Scotland there is another popular belief – that a Pictish king saw a white cross on a blue sky, which was a promise of victory given by St Andrew. It is from this vision that the Scottish saltire, the flag with a blue ground and a white cross, is supposed to be derived. We shall see that this tradition too must be rejected, once we have looked at the actual source that is our earliest evidence for the story, the foundation legend of the church and burgh of St Andrews.

How the cult of St Andrew was established, on the site, Kinrymont in Fife, which was to come to bear the saint's name, was told in this legend. It combined the tale of a Pictish king, 'Ungus' or 'Hungus', who won a victory enjoying the help of St Andrew, with the tale of a religious figure, St Regulus, who, in the fourth or fifth century, brought some of St Andrew's bones to Fife from the east, from Patras or from Constantinople. The happy coincidence of the meeting of the two, the king and the holy man, both devoted to St Andrew, led to the dedication of a church to the saint at Kinrymont.

There are two main versions of this legend, with substantial differences. One, which we may call Version A, can be studied from three sources: a manuscript of the late twelfth century, held in the British Museum; a manuscript of about 1360, written in York but now in Paris; and a printed text put out in 1639 by Archbishop James Ussher in a collection of early religious writings relating to the Church in Britain. Various expressions in the language show that this version was certainly originally written in St Andrews, and it is thought to date from the early twelfth century, though the story in essence may go back considerably further. It is in Latin.

What we may call Version B is found in a British Museum manuscript based on the lost *registrum*, or set of documents, of the St Andrews Priory, and in two texts closely related to it in a fourteenth-century manuscript now in Wolfenbüttel in Germany. The foundation legend is followed in these manuscripts by an account of the recent history and state of affairs of the church at St Andrews, by a man who was an Augustinian canon there. This was written in the lifetime of King David I, that is, before 1153. The writer, who uses Latin throughout, claims that he has simply copied the legend itself from 'old books of the Picts', and this 'copy' closes with the statement that it was composed for a king of the Picts called Ferat, son of Bargoit. This Ferat, according to the regnal lists, was king about AD 840. It has been suggested that there may indeed be a Pictish substratum to the legend as we have it, but what it contained remains doubtful.

It seems, however, that we can say that versions of the legend were in existence by 1100 or so at the latest. They were known to later chroniclers and churchmen; Fordun and Bower used Version B, and Bishop Elphinstone made use of both versions in compiling different sections of his Breviary.

These texts give rise to many problems, and they are only now getting the thorough scholarly attention they deserve. (It is particularly to be hoped that before long they will be available in English!) Both versions of the legend attribute a major role to a Pictish king, and we have seen that there is a historical plausibility in supposing that the 'Angus' who ruled AD 730–61 (i.e. in the eighth century) was the man who introduced the cult of St Andrew to his kingdom. The legend serenely ignores the fundamental chronological absurdity of bringing together such a Pictish king and a holy man bringing relics to Scotland in the fourth or fifth century. The difficulty increases if we suppose that Angus II (AD 820–34) was the king involved.

For our purposes we do not need to discuss in detail, or attempt to explain, the St Regulus part of the story. It obviously derives from the need to account for the presence of relics in the shrine of the apostle at St Andrews: to show how bones of the saint could have got to Scotland. There may have been a wish to cover up or 'replace' a tradition of relics having been brought from Hexham, or in any way through England or the English Church, from which the Scottish Establishment was anxious to disassociate itself.

That there surely were bones in the shrine of St Andrew in medieval times is important, and I shall be referring again to this evidence much later on in this study. However, when the bones came there, where they came from, whose they were – these questions will probably never have a satisfactory answer, and I do not think the actual St Regulus legend has any obvious relevance to our present enquiry about St Andrew's cross.

The King Angus (Ungus/Hungus) part of the story does, however, have relevance, as we shall see. The versions of the legend give very different accounts of the actions of the king, and even differ in the description of the enemies who were facing him: 'Britannicae nationes' in Version A, 'Adhelstanus Rex Saxonum' in Version B and a group of his own 'magnates' ('lords') conspiring against him in Elphinstone's Breviary. The name Adhelstanus represents 'Athelstan', a name used in the royal house of Wessex in England, but it does not seem possible to identify a historical Athelstan who can be plausibly supposed to have fought against Angus I of the Picts, or Angus II.

However, whatever their problems and differences, all the versions refer to help given to the king by St Andrew, and it is important to note exactly what is said in the different texts.

In Version A we are told that 'King Ungus' was surrounded by his enemies, and was walking one day with seven dear companions when

a bright light from heaven surrounded them, and they fell upon their faces, for they could not stand the light. Then a voice was heard from the sky, saying 'Ungus, Ungus, listen to me, who am apostle of Christ, Andrew by name. I have been sent to defend you and keep you safe. Get up, and see the sign of the cross of Christ [*signum crucis Christi*] which stands there, in the sky, and which will go before you against your enemies. And give a tenth part of your inheritance as alms to almighty God, and in honour of St Andrew, his apostle.' On the third day, following this divine counsel, the king divided his army into thirteen bands, and the image of the cross went before each group, and a heavenly light shone from the top of each standard. So they won the day and gave thanks to almighty God and to St Andrew the apostle.

In Version B we are told that the night before he engaged in battle 'Hungus king of the Picts' was asleep and

the blessed Andrew appeared to him and said that he himself, the apostle, would the next day so completely overcome the enemy army that Hungus would triumph over his foes. Hungus said to him, 'Who are you? and where do you come from?' The blessed Andrew replied, 'I am Andrew, apostle of Christ, and I have come now from heaven, sent by God to tell you that tomorrow I shall defeat your enemies and subject them to you, and you will have a joyous victory and return home safely with your army, and my remains will be brought to your kingdom, and the place to which they are brought, with honour and reverence, will be famous to the very end of time.'

Then the king awoke and told his men what the blessed Andrew had revealed to him in his sleep. The Pictish people rejoiced at this, and swore an oath that they would for ever diligently honour St Andrew if those things of which he had spoken to the king came to pass. The next day, encouraged by the promise of the apostle, they prepared for battle; they divided their army and set seven columns around their king. The Saxons also split up their force, and mustered fourteen columns around Adhelstan. When the battle began, the Saxons were straightway deprived of all their valour, and, as God willed, and with the holy apostle Andrew on the side of the Picts, they were turned to flight.

The text in the Aberdeen Breviary in general follows Version A. The king and his companions were walking together and a bright light came upon them and they fell to the ground:

> The king heard a voice from heaven: 'I am Andrew, apostle of Jesus Christ, and I have been sent to defend you from your enemies. Rouse your army and you will win a glorious palm of victory, and as a mark of this the sign of the cross of Christ [*crucis Christi signum*] will continue to go before you in the sky'. The king was roused and the next day he gathered his army and divided it into thirteen bands and the sign of the cross went before each part in a blaze of light. So they made a fierce attack on the enemy.

St Andrew, then, figures in all these versions, but in none of them is there anything that can be taken as a reference to his *own* cross of crucifixion (whether X-shaped or not).

I wrote above that the St Andrews legend was known to the early Scottish chroniclers. The most important of these is Walter Bower who lived from 1385 to 1449, and who wrote a work which he called the *Scotichronicon*. The early part of this is taken almost entirely from a previous writer, John de Fordun. In the 1360s this man collected the material to put together a detailed chronicle of the history of the peoples and kings of Scotland, down to the death of David I in 1153, and a more scrappy account of the next 200 years. These chronicles, of Fordun and Bower, were written in Latin; the text of Bower has only recently become easily accessible in English.

Bower attributes the institution of the cult of St Andrew to a king he calls Hungus (who in fact Bower identifies with the king I have been referring to as Angus II, not Angus I). Bower places the battle, against those he calls 'the Angles', under Athelstan, at a place 'two miles from Haddington, which is now called Athelstaneford'. (This is the site which is today, unfortunately, celebrated as the birthplace of the saltire.)

Bower (Book 4, ch. 14) says that the king and his army were surrounded by their enemies and could see no way of salvation:

So they sought that divine guidance which never fails those who ask with sincerity, and individuals of both high and low degree made humble prayers to God and his saints and especially to St Andrew the Apostle, while the king with a solemn vow promised that, in honour of God and the blessed virgin Mary, he would give a tenth part of his kingdom to blessed Andrew, if he returned safely with his army to his own land and escaped without harm from the power of such a numerous and proud people.

The next night blessed Andrew appeared to the king and said 'God who is ruler above all kings, and who listens always to the pleas of the lowly, has at my intercession heard your prayer, and he will give you tomorrow a joyful victory. He will cast your enemies down before you, and they will not prevail in the fight, for an angel bearing the standard of the cross of the Lord will go before you in the sight of many [*dominicae crucis angelus vexillifer . . . te precedet*]. And you, when you return successfully to your kingdom, be not forgetful of your vow, and do not delay in performing that which you decided of your own will and freely promised to do.'

Bower goes on to describe the change of heart, the new confidence of Hungus and his men, and their complete victory, with the death of Athelstan. He does not refer again to the 'standard' of the cross. Nor does he describe any 'sign of the cross' actually going before each troop of the king's army. And we note that he does not specifically refer to a vision in the sky.

Bower's angel is described as '*vexillum*-carrying'. Now 'vexillum' actually means 'flag'; I do not know if Bower was thinking of a banner or flag made of material here, or whether we should not press the word, and should accept that his account can be taken as referring to a battle standard in the form of a pole with a device on the top, as Version A of the legend might suggest.

So far, then, we have not found any reference mentioning a *cross of St Andrew* in the telling of this legend. When did this come into the story? I suspect we have to lay the blame on Hector Boece, first Principal of King's College in Aberdeen, who in 1526 published a *Chronicle of Scotland*. This contained much fabulous material, and has been regarded as an altogether unreliable source. Boece, in describing the battle under 'King Hungus' says that the Picts shouted 'Saint Andrew our patron be our guide', a phrase reminiscent of what was engraved on the Great Seal of Scotland in 1286 – which I shall discuss later – 'ANDREA SCOTIS DUX ESTO COMPATRIOTIS'. He also said that a cross was seen in the sky 'like the one on which St Andrew died'. This is the earliest text I have found which makes this claim.

Incidentally, the earliest artistic representation of this version of the story that I know of is in the St Andrew cycle painted by Frans Pourbus, which is in St Bavon's Cathedral in Ghent, and which dates from 1572, fifty or so years later than Boece's book. The last panel here, as the Latin text beneath it explains, shows a Scottish king urging his men to victory, inspired by a vision of the cross of St Andrew. This is *not* a white cross on a blue sky; it is a very small dark grey cross, hard to make out against the grey clouds in the corner of the picture!

Boece was writing long after St Andrew had been accepted as the 'patron' of the Scottish people, and long after it had come to be believed that the saint died on an X-shaped cross. So maybe it was an understandable, if regrettably careless, supposition by Boece that if St Andrew wanted to give an encouraging sign to the Picts he would have used the image of his own cross.

It is perhaps worth making the point that *Bower* did not so distort the legend, though of course even by his time the X-shaped cross had been long accepted as St Andrew's. We should also, in noting that the actual legend does not refer to the sign of the cross of St Andrew, ask: when the legend itself took shape had it already come to be believed that St Andrew *had* a special form of cross? If so, then apparently the legend itself was strong enough to resist such distortion in St Andrew's favour!

It is, however, of interest and importance also to ask: where did this element in the story come from? What is the meaning of this reference in Version A to the 'sign of the cross of Christ' appearing in the sky, and going before the bands of soldiers, and is there significance in Bower's account of an angel bearing a standard with the cross of Christ on it?

A striking parallel to the Angus story is the experience of the Roman Emperor Constantine the Great before the Battle of the Milvian Bridge outside Rome in AD 312. The main sources for this are Lactantius and Eusebius. Lactantius, in *On the Death of the Persecutors* (ch. 44), says that Constantine was warned in a dream to mark the sign of God on his helmet and on his men's shields. The sign meant by Lactantius, it is clear, was not a simple cross but the chi-rho monogram, which was made up from the forms of the first two letters of the word 'Christ' in Greek – XP.

Eusebius, in his *History of the Church*, says Constantine attributed victory over Maxentius to the 'saving sign' (of the cross of Christ). At the end of his life, however, the emperor privately told Eusebius more of what happened in AD 312, as he remembered it, or wanted to remember it, and Eusebius records this in his *Life of Constantine* (ch. 28–31). The emperor said that he and his army had been on the march and had seen a cross of light superimposed on the sun, and the words 'By this, conquer' written in the sky. The following night Christ had appeared in a vision with the sign, and told Constantine to make a copy of it for his standard in war. Constantine had then had made a tall pole with a wreath of gold surmounting it enclosing the chi-rho monogram.

16. 'Centenionalis' coin of Constantine the Great, AD 327, showing standard ('labarum') with chi-rho (From: Kent, *Roman Coins*, © Hirmer Verlag, Munich)

From this it is generally agreed that the 'sign' Constantine adopted was the chi-rho, and that it was this that was fashioned on the top of the standards of his army. It is shown as such on coins. The chi-rho became a very popular Christian symbol from the middle of the fourth century.

It seems to me possible that the tradition about Constantine was made use of by King Angus himself. He could have had battle standards made with the chi-rho sign – or perhaps a simple cross – on the top. These would have gone before the several divisions of his army, as the legend seems to suggest. And this would have been presented as a heaven-inspired and morale-boosting decision. The vision, the dream, perhaps indeed the whole legend, may have been worked up later. But I think the idea that it was inspired by the Constantinian precedent should be taken seriously.

We know very little about the Picts, and our ignorance has tended to find expression in a reluctance to take them seriously as a sophisticated, cultured people. This has been so in spite of the evidence from Pictish monuments, the carved stones, that they were capable of considerable artistic achievement, and that their society was one of developed structures, finding meaningful expression in these monuments. Archaeological investigations are filling out the picture in other ways, and we are beginning to see the Picts, not as some wild barbarians beyond the lands of civilisation, but as a people with regular contact with their neighbours and involved in an interchange of influences, a part of that wider civilised world.

We saw that Bede tells us how King Nechtan had approached churchmen in Northumbria and had adopted the ways of the 'Roman' Church and had instituted the cult of St Peter. I would have thought that this is an indication of increasing interest among Pictish learned men in ecclesiastical and secular history. Also, alongside the movements north and south of armies, as recorded in the scanty chronicles of the times, there was surely growing trade and travel bringing Picts into contact with the south of Britain and the Continent.

It does not seem to me difficult to suppose that Picts of the time of a King Angus, whether he was of the ninth or even of the eighth century, knew a good deal about the Roman Emperor Constantine. They would have seen advantages in taking him as a model, investing their own king with something of his great majesty and power. It is intriguing, to say the least, that a brother of Angus II was called Constantine, and that there were later kings of that name.

It should be remembered of course that a particular reason for the Roman Constantine to be renowned in Britain was that he served there under his father, one of the imperial rulers or 'Augusti'. They actually fought against the Picts. When his father died at York in AD 306 Constantine was their acclaimed emperor in his stead.

A possibility of course is that the legend of the cross in the sky does not go right back to the time of the King Angus with whom it is associated, but that the whole story, with its derivation from the Constantinian precedent, was invented for the greater glory of that Pictish king some time afterwards.

To sum up, this investigation of the St Andrews foundation legend has shown that there was an interest in St Andrew among the Picts, and that it was believed a church in his name had been founded in the time of a King Angus, in the eighth or ninth century. The creators of the legend say nothing about the saint having a special X-shaped cross, and may themselves not have been aware of any tradition that he died on one.

However, they transmitted (or themselves invented?) the part of the story that has the Pictish king recognising and perhaps using some Christian symbol as a sign of divine favour, whether this was a simple 'cross' or a 'chi-rho'. The possibility that this in itself could have been what was responsible for crediting St Andrew with a cross of crucifixion shaped like an X will be taken up later – and is my justification for this rather long discussion of the possible parallel with the vision of Emperor Constantine the Great.

# 9

## *British Representations of St Andrew's Martyrdom*

The best artefact to look at first now we are coming to consider how the death of St Andrew was shown in our British material is the Scottish 'Seal of the Guardians' of 1286. This is because the depiction is unambiguous and the date is certain.

In March 1286 King Alexander III of Scotland died after a fall from his horse, when riding on a stormy night near Kinghorn in Fife. He was only forty-four and had married for the second time in the previous year. As it was, however, since his two sons by his first wife, Margaret, daughter of King Henry III of England, were already dead, he left as his recognised heir his granddaughter Margaret, the 'Maid of Norway', who was only four years old. The great men of Church and State met at Scone and appointed six 'Guardians' who swore to preserve the land of Scotland for Queen Margaret. The six comprised the bishops of St Andrews and Glasgow, and two earls and two barons, who reflected different geographical and established family interests.

The Guardians had to have designed and produced a 'great seal' to replace the royal seal of King Alexander, for use on important documents as their symbol of legitimate authority. On one side of this seal was shown the royal arms with the rampant lion, together with the legend, SIGILLUM SCOCIE DEPUTATUM REGIMINI REGNI, 'the seal of Scotland appointed for the government of the kingdom'. On the other side was St Andrew on an X-shaped cross, with ropes, also forming X shapes, holding his wrists and ankles, and with the appeal, ANDREA SCOTIS DUX ESTO COMPATRIOTIS, 'Andrew be leader of your fellow Scots'.

17. Seal of the Guardians of Scotland, from matrix of 1286. British Library, seal xxxiv. 48 (By permission of the British Library)

I believe this is the earliest certain evidence for the adoption of St Andrew as pre-eminent patron of the Scottish people, a truly national patron saint. It seems that Scotland was one of the first nations, if not *the* first, to adopt a national saint, overriding and subsuming all the loyalties to the existing patron saints of particular churches, localities, royal dynasties and great families. The position of St Andrew was consolidated in the coming struggle with England, which in its turn established St George as undisputed patron saint of the English people.

St Andrew as a unifying figure for the Scottish nation was, I think, the 'establishment' choice, rather than a 'popular' one, which might have fixed on St Columba. It was due at least in part to the powerful influence at the time of the church at St Andrews itself and its head, Bishop William Fraser, one of the Guardians. St Andrew – brother of St Peter, and one who could be presented as the champion of Christianity in Scotland through the presence of his relics at St Andrews – did indeed prove a useful political figurehead in the struggle for independence of State and Church, and Scottish attempts to get papal backing for their claims.

In 1286, then, as the seal shows, St Andrew was believed, in Scotland, to have died on an X-shaped cross. The saint was also shown thus on a seal of Bishop William Fraser himself, and earlier than this the counter seal of Bishop Gamelin of St Andrews (1255–71) had St Andrew being tied to an X-shaped cross by two executioners. The seal of Prior John Haddington (1264–1304) showed the saint on the X-cross, with an angel each side of him. From at least the middle of the thirteenth century, therefore, it seems that it was believed in St Andrews that St Andrew died on this special shape of cross.

Other churches in Britain dedicated to St Andrew produced seals with a portrayal of the saint. We have evidence of this from the use of seals on surviving documents or from actual seal matrices. A seal of the Abbey of Owston (or

18. Replica of seal of Prior John of Haddington, 1264–1304. St Andrews Cathedral Museum (© Crown copyright, reproduced courtesy of Historic Scotland)

19. Thirteenth-century seal of the Dean and Chapter of Wells Cathedral. British Library, seal lvi. 65 (By permission of the British Library)

20. Counter seal of Bishop Richard of Rochester, 1238–50. British Library, seal eg.ch. 376 (By permission of the British Library)

Osulveston) in Leicestershire has St Andrew being tied by two men to such a cross; it is dated to the thirteenth century. A similar date is given to a seal of Grimstone and Yetminster in the Diocese of Salisbury. The church there was dedicated to St Andrew and he is shown on the seal spreadeagled in an X shape with foliage around. An actual *cross* is not clear here, but is surely meant to be understood. St Andrew on his X cross appears on a thirteenth-century seal of the Dean and Chapter of Wells Cathedral.

Particularly interesting are seals associated with Rochester Cathedral; this we saw was an early dedication by St Augustine in the name of St Andrew. A counter seal of a Bishop of Rochester, Richard of Wendover, shows St Andrew on an X cross. Around the device is an inscription – partially lost – which can be reconstructed to read ME IUVET ANDREAS QUEM CONSUL VINXIT EGEAS – 'Help me Andrew, you who were bound by the consul Egeas'. Richard was bishop at Rochester from 1238 to 1250. This must be one of the earliest seals anywhere, of which evidence still survives, to show the saint on the X cross.

A Rochester document of 1459 in the British Library has a seal

21. Seal of Rochester Cathedral with legend 'ego crucis Christi servus sum'. British Library, seal colf.ch. iv. 53 (By permission of the British Library)

showing St Andrew being tied to his X cross by two men. In Birch's Catalogue it is said that this seal actually comes from a matrix (mould) of the thirteenth century. This seal is especially interesting because it has the inscription round it EGO CRUCIS CHRISTI SERVUS SUM – 'I am the servant of the cross of Christ'. This reminds us of the traditional particular association of St Andrew with 'the cross' of Christ's redemption.

The device of St Andrew on this cross was used in many later seals created for the use of ecclesiastical authorities or private individuals. A similar device was used on Scottish coins from the time of Robert III, around 1400. There also developed the practice of showing the saint, not being crucified, but holding an X cross, and then, presumably later when the iconography had become familiar, the practice of using the X cross by itself, to be understood as a symbol of St Andrew, and indeed by transference of Scotland. The earliest clear written reference I know of to this symbolic use is in an Act of the Scottish Parliament of 1385, where Scottish soldiers and their French allies are directed to wear, as a distinguishing mark on their fronts and backs, a white cross of St Andrew on a black background. Similarly, in 1386 the English army was directed to wear the red cross of St George.

However, I need at this point to draw attention to what have been thought to be early examples of this 'symbolic' use of the X on ecclesiastical seals. A device used over several centuries, with some variations, by the Chapter of St Andrews Priory shows a church building, thought to represent the early cathedral, which became the Church of St Rule later. On one side of the tower is shown an upright equal-armed, 'Greek' cross, and on the other an X shape which is universally described as a 'saltire', and generally assumed to represent the cross of St Andrew. The earliest example of this type of seal dates from about 1180. If this symbol is meant to refer to a cross of crucifixion then it is being used well *before* St Andrew is being shown in Scotland actually being put to death on such a cross. I find this puzzling and unlikely, and I shall discuss these seals more fully later, together with possibly comparable evidence from England.

I wrote earlier that the Rohault book on the iconography of saints took notice of British material about St Andrew, and it contains illustrations of a number of the seals I have already discussed. There is also a drawing of a French seal of 1256, from Avranches. This shows St Andrew lying crossways, but with legs together, across the seal. There is a superficial likeness to crucifixion on an X cross, but a close look at the seal proves that the cross behind the figure of the saint is a Latin cross, shown on a slant. So

22.   Thirteenth-century seal from Avranches, France (From: Rohault, *Les Saints de la Messe*)

here we have a suggestive difference between French and British seals of the mid thirteenth century.

Somewhat similar to these seals as artefacts are the metal badges that were acquired by pilgrims to the shrine of St Andrew. They were not usually of intrinsic value and are often rather crudely executed objects, but they were like talismans probably thought to give the protection of the saint on the way, and maybe they had to be produced, for example, at ferry crossings. They were the proof of a pilgrimage vowed and made – rather more serious mementoes of a journey than the modern souvenir plate or car sticker! The badges were designed with holes, for stitching to garments, and they were made of an alloy of tin and lead, and cast in stone moulds. Ten or so different pilgrim badges featuring St Andrew have been found, showing him spread out in an X shape, sometimes with the cross actually visible, and occasionally with an executioner each side (as often on the seals). They date from the thirteenth to the sixteenth century.

Several of these badges have been found in the London area. I have wondered if these could relate to pilgrimages to Rochester rather than to St Andrews, but I think this is rather unlikely. The most famous and miracle-working shrine in Rochester Cathedral in the Middle Ages was that of St William of Perth, a Scot who was murdered at Rochester in 1201.

There are some examples of Andrew badges from Scotland itself: a mould for a badge, found at North Berwick, half of a fine badge found at Castlecliffe, St Andrews, and one discovered in Perth, in a pit with contents dated 1250–1300 (plate 12).

Perhaps earlier than any of the seals or badges showing the X-shaped cross is a manuscript now in the Pierpont Morgan Library in New York, the Huntingfield Psalter. This has a page showing the martyrdoms of four apostles, Peter, Paul, Andrew and James. Peter is shown crucified upside down, Paul and James are about to be beheaded, and Andrew is shown being tied to a large X-shaped cross (plate 13). This Psalter is dated to 1210–20, and is thought to have been the work of an English artist. It was certainly in the possession of the Huntingfield family in Essex in the thirteenth century. (St Andrew appears in an earlier English manuscript, a troper from the third quarter of the eleventh century, but here he is shown seated, holding a long cross-topped staff.)

The wonderful Macclesfield Psalter of about 1320, recently acquired for the nation, and now in the Fitzwilliam Museum, Cambridge, has been associated with the Church of St Andrew, Gorleston, Suffolk. At the beginning it has two illuminations, one of St Edmund and one of St Andrew, who is delicately holding a thin X-shaped cross by his right side, with what seems to be a book in his upraised left hand (plate 14).

Even earlier than the Huntingfield Psalter is a wall painting, said to be of the twelfth century, in Ickleton Church, Cambridgeshire. This shows a figure with his arms spread as on an X-shaped cross, with men each side apparently tying him on, as in so many representations of St Andrew's martyrdom. Alongside him are shown the martyrdoms of St Peter (upside down) and St Laurence, and above are scenes of the Passion of Christ. The paintings here were only discovered in 1981 when plaster was removed during restoration work after a fire. The lower part of the Andrew figure is covered up by a later monument fixed to the wall, so we cannot see the bottom half of the X cross, but I believe the identification is right. We shall find that, with a twelfth-century date, this must be among the earliest portrayals anywhere of St Andrew on an X-shaped cross (plate 16).

From the thirteenth and early fourteenth century are other wall paintings that show St Andrew in this way. A particularly interesting example is a mural that was in St John's, Winchester. It is now lost, but is known from a detailed copy. St Andrew is here tied to an X cross next to Christ shown nailed to a Latin cross. There is 'Franciscan' influence in the painting, and, partly because of this, the work has been dated to about 1250. In the Galilee Porch of Durham Cathedral there is an arcade with paintings dated to about 1300 that show a central crucifixion scene, with martyrdoms of apostles on either side. To the right is the execution of St Paul, and next to him St Andrew, plainly on an X-shaped cross. A painting in Rochester Cathedral has been claimed to show Andrew, but is said now to be too faded for the figure to be identified.

In the thirteenth-century buildings of Lacock Abbey in Wiltshire there are wall paintings including a partially pre-served figure which must be St Andrew, tied (and nailed?) to an X-shaped cross. This, with the painting of St Christopher nearby, had been authoritatively dated to about 1275, but a more recent researcher places the Andrew painting later, in the fifteenth century.

There was a tradition that what we know as 'the Apostles' Creed' was created by the individual apostles contributing sentences. Peter is always given the first sentence: 'I believe in Almighty God', and Andrew is often, but not always, given the second: 'And in his Son . . .' Longthorpe Tower, which is near Peterborough, has a number of well-preserved and im-portant wall paintings. Among these is a series of the apostles, shown with their 'creed sentences'. Peter carries a scroll bearing his sentence, and also keys, while Andrew, as well as a scroll with the second sentence, also carries a small and slender 'saltire cross' in his left hand. The most obvious interpretation of this is that it is a symbol of his martyrdom on an X-shaped cross. These paintings are dated to about 1330. As we have seen, there is plenty of local material to show that by that time it was believed in Britain that St Andrew had died on such a cross.

A good example of a 'creed window', with the apostles shown with their sentences in stained glass, is to be seen in the Church of St Laurence, Ludlow. Here Andrew is shown, half-length, holding quite a large, but very thin, X-shaped cross. This I am sure is to be understood as a reference to his crucifixion, and not as simply a 'cross' symbolising his Christian devotion. This is not surprising; I believe the window is not earlier than the fifteenth century.

In moving on from the evidence in wall painting in Britain to other representations of St Andrew in glass, I should perhaps first remind the reader of the window in Greystoke Church, near Penrith, which I described briefly in Chapter 1. We saw that this was designed to tell the story of Andrew's adventures in the east, and it did not contain any scene of the saint's martyrdom. I have also referred to the window in Canterbury

23. St Andrew in 'creed window', in Church of St Laurence, Ludlow
(Reproduced courtesy of the Rector and Church Wardens)

Cathedral that shows Andrew being put to death on a tree. We have to remember that this glass has only recently come to Britain, and was certainly not made in Britain in the first place. It is therefore not relevant to our argument here.

We saw earlier that St Wilfrid built a church in St Andrew's name at Hexham. There is no early glass in that church, but in his church at Ripon, now the cathedral, dedicated to St Peter and St Wilfrid, there is a window made up of medallions, which were formerly in the great east window, and which date from 1300 or soon after. One of these medallions shows St Paul, holding the sword by which he was beheaded. Another has St Andrew with his arms and legs spread wide, as on an X-shaped cross. No actual cross is visible, and there are no other figures in this small scene.

In York Minster there are four noteworthy representations of St Andrew in pre-1400 glass. The 'bell-founders window' of the early fourteenth century has in its tracery three four-lobed roundels showing St Peter with keys, St Paul with a sword, and St Andrew holding a small thin X-shaped cross. In the tracery of a window dated to 1338 in the north aisle there are three similar roundels, showing Christ enthroned, Peter crucified upside down, and Andrew with his arms spread as on an X-shaped cross. His legs are shown rather as if he is walking, but I think we should accept this as meant to be a representation of the saint on his X cross. In a mid fourteenth-century clerestory window in the choir Andrew is shown as a half-length figure, carrying in one hand a book and in the other a very small thin X cross. This undoubtedly represents his cross of martyrdom, because the saint is one of a row of martyrs, all with their instruments of death: St Matthias with an axe, St Paul with a sword and St Bartholomew with a flaying knife (and his own skin). St John also appears, but with an eagle and a palm; he did not die a martyr's violent death.

The only full scene of St Andrew's martyrdom in York Minster is in the 'Mauley Window'. Some of this is modern, but the original glass is of the fourteenth century. Andrew is shown being tied to a structure by two men on ladders. We can see the lower part of an X cross to which his legs are tied, and his arms are spread wide above his head, though the design here is not so clear (plate 15). Anyway, there can be no doubt that from soon after 1300 at least it was believed by artists and presumably clerics at York that St Andrew died on an X-shaped cross.

Another window in the Minster is claimed to represent the martyrdom of St Vincent. Here there is a man with arms spread wide, and his feet together, but with what appears to be the bottom part of an X structure below them. A man on each side seems to attack the figure. Other martyrdoms shown in this window are those of St Laurence, St Stephen – these two often associated with St Vincent – and St Edmund. The glass is dated to the early fourteenth century.

We have now noticed a number of examples of stained glass where St Andrew is shown, not being martyred, but with a small cross as a symbol of his martyrdom. This continued to be a way of designating the saint, especially when he appeared with other apostles and holy men. In the east window of Exeter Cathedral he appears holding a small X cross in front of his chest. The date here is later fourteenth century. We shall find examples too of this form of representation in thirteenth/fourteenth-century sculpture, and also in embroidery, which is the medium I next discuss.

One of the glories of English medieval achievement is its embroidery, remarkable both for its technical skill and for its artistry. Everyone is familiar with the Bayeux Tapestry (so-called), which was almost certainly produced in England. This, although made for display in a church, had a secular, political purpose. Most of the other surviving material is ecclesiastic, and although there are fine examples to be seen in Britain, made as vestments for the church here, it is clear that many items were made for churches on the Continent, and a number of these survive, mostly from the fourteenth century. They take the form of chasubles (round vestments with a hole for the head), copes (long semi-circular sleeveless cloak-like vestments), and orphreys (ornate border strips edging such garments).

The earliest example of a St Andrew shown in English church embroidery is a figure on the surviving part of a stole,

which was used as a shroud for the body of Bishop William of
Worcester, buried in 1236. The stole itself is thought to have
been at least a hundred years old at the time. On it were panels
with figures of the apostles, who are named, and among these is
Andrew. The apostles hold a book in one hand and stretch out
the other. The only one surviving shown with an instrument of
martyrdom is St Paul, with a sword.

Two fine examples of English work are in the Victoria and
Albert Museum in London, the Syon Cope and the Steeple
Aston Cope. The former dates from about 1300. On it are
embroidered angels and figures of saints, and among these is
one that is surely St Andrew. He is holding over his right arm

24. Figure of St Andrew on early fourteenth-century Steeple Aston cope, now in
V&A Museum (Photo: V&A Images, Victoria and Albert Museum, London)

a small thin cross, appearing as X-shaped. The Steeple Aston Cope was at some stage cut into pieces, and it is a large rectangular section of it that is on display in the museum. The work is now badly faded, but the details can be studied in splendidly clear plate photographs. The cope has portrayals of many saints, with trails of foliage embroidered around the scenes, and lions in the gaps between. Among the saints included are St Peter, shown being crucified upside down; St Laurence, with a small gridiron; and St Margaret, emerging from the back of a dragon. So, there are examples included here both of actual martyrdoms, and of a martyr depicted with a symbol of his martyrdom. In the case of St Andrew the saint is identified by his name, in abbreviated form, S ĀDEAS, and he is shown being tied by two men to an X-shaped cross. The date of this cope is given as early fourteenth century, so it may be later than the Syon Cope, which, as we have seen, already shows the X-cross as a small symbol of Andrew's death, not realistically as the physical instrument of his martyrdom.

The authoritative book on English medieval embroidery gives details of three works, now on the Continent, which were made in England, and which show St Andrew actually being crucified on an X-shaped cross. One dates from about 1350, the other two from about 1300. One of these is particularly interesting. It is now in the possession of St John Lateran in Rome. The tradition is that Pope Boniface VIII wore it there in 1300. Its English origin has never been questioned, and is confirmed by the fact that among the saints depicted on it are St Thomas of Canterbury and St Edmund, king and martyr.

Continental churches or museums also hold six or so examples of work thought to be English and mostly dated 1300–50, which show St Andrew holding an X-shaped cross, like the one on the Syon Cope. There is one thought to be earlier, from around 1260, now in Rome. It resembles the Syon Cope, but the thin X cross held by St Andrew is very much larger.

Perhaps earlier than any of the embroidery I have just been describing is what is known as the Uppsala Cope. It is said to have been acquired for celebrations connected with the foundation of the cathedral at Uppsala and the honouring of the local Swedish saint, King Erik, and its creation is dated to the mid thirteenth century. The interesting thing here is that a figure named as S ANDREAS on this cope is shown being tied by two men to a *Latin* cross. This is one example at variance with all the other evidence from English embroidery, and it is to be noted that experts have some doubt about the provenance of this cope. Although the style and technique seem 'English' there are features of the cope that have led some to think it was made in France. (Incidentally, these experts do not use as an item in their argument how St Andrew is represented.) Of course I would myself find it interesting if it could be shown that this cope was made by people on the Continent who had perhaps not caught up with the 'new' idea that St Andrew died on an X-shaped cross!

To complete this discussion of how St Andrew's martyrdom and his cross are shown in British art I turn to representations in carving and sculpture. I have already referred to the shaft of a cross at Auckland St Andrew, of around AD 800, which has a figure tied to an upright cross that is almost certainly St Andrew. I have also mentioned the identification of the saint (not on a cross, though) as one of the figures on a Pictish stone, also of about 800, found at Portmahomack, near Tain.

Of the thirteenth century, the period to which much of the material I have already described in this chapter belongs, is a prominent sculpture of St Andrew at Peterborough Cathedral. The early church on this site was dedicated in the name of St Peter, but in the thirteenth century the cathedral was consecrated in the names of St Peter, St Paul and St Andrew. Seated figures of these three saints are to be seen high up in the gables of the west front, built by 1237. The statues are badly eroded (St Peter has 'dropped his keys' says the Cathedral Guide), and it is not possible to be certain whether the St Andrew was portrayed as carrying a small cross, or other attribute. (I shall describe later an unusual seal from Peterborough which has the saint with his cross.)

Another English statue of St Andrew is on the tower of Worcester Cathedral. There is a drawing of such a statue,

25. Figure on the tower of Worcester Cathedral. Compare Rohault drawing, fig. 5 (Photo: C. Guy. Reproduced by permission of the Chapter of Worcester Cathedral)

shown carrying a small X-shaped cross, in Rohault, where the figure is dated to the thirteenth century, and the drawing of it is attributed to 'M. Wild'. This man wrote an Architect's Report on the state of repair works to the tower and other parts of the cathedral in 1867, with some illustrations. In correspondence with me the authorities at Worcester were doubtful if such a statue of St Andrew still existed, but they were able in the end to identify one of the existing statues on the tower as the St Andrew of Wild's drawing. It has suffered more deterioration, and perhaps some restoration, but it is possible to see that the figure did originally carry a small cross.

Incidentally, at Worcester there is also a Victorian statue of St Andrew in the north porch, and a figure of St Andrew in a chantry chapel, which is of the sixteenth century, and which has to show the saint with a very much squashed-up X cross!

We have seen that already in the thirteenth century St Andrew could be shown in various other British media holding a small cross, as at Worcester.

When I was writing about the representations of St Andrew's martyrdom on the Continent I maintained that (except for the particularly early, and therefore puzzling, capital from Quercy) it was only from around the beginning of the fourteenth century that we have examples of his death actually being shown there, in any media, as occurring on an X-shaped cross. However, it is interesting that certainly from early in that century there are also examples from the Continent of St Andrew *holding* such a cross, rather than the Latin cross he holds in sculptures on French cathedrals in the thirteenth century. For example, there is a statue in Cologne Cathedral showing the saint thus. It dates from about 1325. There is a similar statue on Freiburg Cathedral in Germany; this is dated to about 1300. What inference do we draw from the appearance of these early examples, on the Continent, as well as in Britain, of an X cross, shown associated with St Andrew, and probably to be understood, not as a symbol of Christ or the Church, but as a symbol of his actual crucifixion?

It is appropriate here to describe two other artefacts that seem to show such early instances of this symbolic cross. One is

the 'Ulrik Altar Frontal' now in Bergen. The painting shows
Christ in Majesty in the centre, with twelve saints, shown in two
rows of three on each side. Of the four figures nearest to Christ
one is shown carrying keys (St Peter), one carrying a sword (St
Paul?), and one carrying a slender X-shaped cross. I believe
this must be St Andrew, though from the illustration I have
seen I have not been able to make out for sure symbolic
'instruments of martyrdom' carried by any of the other figures.
The date of this frontal is given as around 1250. The style is
related to the 'sculptural mannerisms' of the Westminster
School of the 1240s, and it has been suggested that the work
might be associated with the visit of Matthew Paris to King
Haakon of Norway in 1248. If an artist from Britain painted
this frontal, it is not perhaps surprising that he showed St
Andrew with such a cross: this iconographical practice being
already established in Britain by then.

The second thing I should like to describe in detail is a wall
painting in Bruges, which I mentioned in an earlier chapter, that
shows St Andrew with an X cross. In the chancel of Onze Lieve
Vrouwekerk there are excavated graves, now to be seen through
glass panels let into the paving. Decorated in a manner found also
elsewhere in Belgium, these rectangular tombs have frescoes on
the inside walls. Usually there is a crucifixion scene on the east
wall and a mother-and-child scene on the west, with angels and
other figures and decorative crosses of various shapes on the long
sides. One of the graves is known to be that of Peter Calf, a church
dignitary, who died in 1295, and this has on one side an angel and
a monk-like figure, and on the other two angels and St Andrew,
shown full-length carrying quite a large and very thin X cross.
This surely must represent his cross of crucifixion (plate 10).

It is especially important that at this early date we have such
Continental instances of the saint, shown, not even realistically
on the X cross, but with it in symbolic form, its meaning
already presumably generally understandable.

To return to the British material, we come finally to one of the
most tantalising pieces of evidence in our survey. An apparently
clear representation of the saint not *with* his X cross but *on* it is to
be found on a font, the 'Cottam font', now in Langtoft Church

near Driffield in Yorkshire. This tub-shaped font has several different scenes around it: Adam and Eve, with the Tree of Knowledge between them; the Tree of Life; St Margaret of Antioch being swallowed by the dragon and emerging from his back; St Laurence lying on a gridiron and being prodded by a man; and a figure generally identified as St Andrew being tied by two men to an X-shaped cross. One commentator has described this scene as being the 'Deposition' (of Christ) from the cross, but this is certainly wrong. However, it should be pointed out that the martyrs on this font are not named; the identification of St Andrew is based entirely on comparison with other representations of his martyrdom that are certain (plate 17).

This font is one of several in East Yorkshire of similar form and decoration: one at North Grimston, not far from Langtoft, and still in use, has on it an ecclesiastic or saint figure and a representation of the Last Supper; another at Cowlam has a female saint, Adam and Eve, two men wrestling, a vivid scene showing the Magi approaching the Virgin and Child, and a king probably meant as Herod.

It is thought that the scenes on these fonts follow carefully worked out themes, to do with redemption and the choice between good and evil, and though the execution varies in quality they should be attributed to one workshop or school of sculptors. There is no documentary evidence to give a date for any one of them. The criteria for dating have to be largely stylistic, and the most detailed recent study I have seen suggests 1130–50 as the period when they were made, with the Cottam font placed late in the sequence. If this is anywhere near right then this font at Langtoft is the earliest representation so far found in Britain of St Andrew actually on the X-shaped cross. (It may be, however, that the Ickleton wall painting will one day be proved to have as good a claim.) This is what makes the question of its date so important. A further point I would like to make, and shall take up again later, is this – it is surely most unlikely that a sculptor of fonts in twelfth-century Yorkshire (or a wall-painter in twelfth-century Cambridgeshire) himself actually 'invented' the idea of showing St Andrew tied to an X-shaped cross, and still less likely that, if he did so, it is from this rather crudely carved humble piece, made for a small village church, that the whole tradition of the X cross sprang. Then where *did* it come from?

Certainly the conclusions we may draw from all this British material are that the idea had come into being at least by AD 1150, that it was fairly quickly and generally adopted in England and Scotland, and that by 1300, and indeed probably some decades earlier, the saint could be shown carrying a small X cross, which would be generally understood as a symbol of his martyrdom.

A further caution I should include here: we may have surviving in Britain an example of St Andrew on an upright cross from about AD 800, and examples of him on an X-shaped cross from 1150 or so, but there are around three and a half blank centuries between. Wherever, and for whatever reason, the X-shaped cross was 'invented', we have to ask: was this shortly before it first appears, on the font, and then on seals, in wall painting, and so on; or could it have had a longer history, in belief and story, if not in art? This question must form part of the tying together of the literary and artistic evidence we have looked at so far, and of the exploration, which can be no more than highly speculative, of possible theories to account for this remarkable, and apparently British, contribution to the tradition and the iconography associated with St Andrew.

However, before we come on to the consideration of how we might explain the appearance of the X-shaped cross associated with St Andrew I want briefly to refer to the evidence for its importance and significance in Burgundian legend and iconography, and ask whether this can contribute to discussion of the problem.

# 10

## *The Burgundian Evidence*

I have already referred to the foundation of the Order of the Golden Fleece by Philip the Good, Duke of Burgundy, in 1429. St Andrew was adopted as patron of the Order, and one of its symbols was an X-shaped cross, usually depicted in red. An increasing familiarity with this emblem contributed to the growing use and eventual dominance on the Continent of the X-shaped cross in connection with St Andrew and in representations of his martyrdom.

It is natural to wonder why the Duke of Burgundy chose this X-cross symbolism; whether there was any reason for it beyond the fact that certainly by the fifteenth century there were already many examples (under influence from Britain?) of this distinctive iconography. Even if this was the explanation it is however perhaps understandable that Burgundian patriots sought something more, to place the origin of the X cross way back in their own past, and so popularised stories of links with St Andrew, much as we have found happened in our own Scottish tradition. Is there anything more substantial to be found in the Burgundian legends and theorising about St Andrew and his cross?

When the Roman Empire was powerful the Burgundians seem to have lived in what is now northern Poland, between the rivers Oder and Vistula. They moved west, as did so many other peoples, and were allowed by the Romans to settle around Lake Geneva in AD 443. From there they moved into the Rhône valley, where they built up an extensive kingdom which enjoyed long periods of independence and prosperity in the early Middle Ages. They then fell under French control, but the creation of Philip the Bold (a son of King John II of

France) as Duke of Burgundy in 1363 brought 'Burgundy' back as a major player on the political scene. It was the grandson of this Philip who instituted the Order of the Golden Fleece.

A historian of the period, Olivier de la Marche (d.1502), wrote of John the Fearless, son of Philip the Bold, adopting the cross of St Andrew as his emblem, and displaying it at a battle in 1408. However, Olivier says that he was merely reviving an ancient loyalty, suppressed in the years of French dominance, because the early Burgundians had always used the St Andrew's cross as their battle standard. Olivier's story is that Mary Magdalen came to Provence fourteen years after the death of Jesus, and converted the king of the Burgundians to Christianity, after bringing back to life his son Stephen. This Stephen became the next king, and brought to Marseilles the actual cross on which St Andrew had died, and took the sign of this cross for his battle standard.

I shall write more below about this and other stories of supposed relics of St Andrew's cross in the Burgundian tradition. Here I need only draw attention to the completely unhistorical way in which Olivier locates 'Burgundians' in Provence several hundred years before they ever reached the Rhône. His work in fact reminds me of that of Hector Boece, making too much of the story of a cross seen in the sky by a Pictish king. Olivier was writing when it was accepted that St Andrew's cross was X-shaped, and he naturally supposed that it had always been believed to be so. I feel entitled to query whether a St Andrew's X-shaped cross was ever waved on a rallying standard in battle in south-eastern France before the time of John the Fearless!

However, a much more recent Burgundian patriot has developed a theory to associate his people with the cross of St Andrew. This has the merit of ingenuity at least! Writing in 1935, Pidoux de la Maduère claimed that the Burgundians brought with them from the east their devotion to St Andrew and the X-shaped cross. He finds the evidence in what he calls 'l'enseigne [official badge] de la légion romaine des Pannonici'. This legion he associates with the Roman province of Pannonia, which he envisages as roughly the region where the

Burgundians lived in the first century AD, and which he equates also with the 'Scythia' where St Andrew was at that time making his converts, among whom could have been these Burgundians. The geography of course does not make any sense at all. The Burgundian tribe lived far to the north and west of any 'Scythia' that Andrew could possibly have visited, and the Roman province of Pannonia was a different place again. It comprised land close to Italy, south of the Danube (modern western Hungary–eastern Austria).

I believe the emblem that De la Maduère suggests represents the cross of St Andrew must be one that is to be found among the many illustrations of civil and military insignia accompanying the Latin text known as the *Notitia Dignitatum*, which indeed De la Maduère gives as his source. This is a list of functionaries of the late Roman Empire. Among men described as commanders are those of infantry units (not 'legions') in the main field army (*magistri peditum*). The badge of one such commander shows what could be taken as an X cross in red on a green-blue ground (or an upright cross in green-blue on a red ground?), set within a red circle (Seeck, p. 155). The unit of infantry in question here is named as the 'Pannoniciani'; I understand these troops served in Italy and Thrace, and presumably they were originally recruited in the province of Pannonia.

De la Maduère's (most implausible) theory, then, is that before coming west Burgundians were converted to Christianity by St Andrew, and even then believed (on what evidence?) that he had died on an X-shaped cross. This cross they got represented as an official Roman military emblem; and later they took with them on their migrations both the worship of St Andrew and the honouring of a red X-shaped cross. The author suggests that when they settled on the Rhône their belief was reinforced by the tradition there of an early cult of St Andrew and the presence of his actual X-shaped cross in the vicinity of Marseilles.

The story of this relic – as of so many – is unsatisfactory, unconvincing and incomplete. One sixteenth-century writer said that the cross was deposited in the Abbey of Saint-Victoire at Marseilles. Other early accounts suggest it was first held at a nunnery, called Véaume, two miles from Marseilles on the coast. (Presumably the cross was supposed to have been acquired and deposited there by that early King Stephen mentioned by Olivier de la Marche.) This nunnery was sacked by the Saracens in the eighth century, and the nuns were massacred, but it is said that they first hid the cross. Nothing was known of its whereabouts until about 1250 when a monk of Saint-Victoire had a vision of an angel who told him where it was. The monk recovered the cross (or large parts of it) and it was then venerated at Saint-Victoire until it was sacrilegiously burnt in 1793. Some fragments were saved, and honoured in a reliquary at the abbey. I presume it is these fragments which were fairly recently gifted by the church at Marseilles to the new Cathedral of St Andrew at Patras.

There is always great suspicion about relics that are 'lost' and 'found'. I think we can safely say that the history of this relic only begins, at the earliest, around 1250. As with the 'bones of St Andrew' in Scotland, we must allow for the invention of a satisfying legend to explain the possession and the origin of the sacred object. As for the relic itself, De la Maduère implies that there are sixteenth- and seventeenth-century descriptions of the Saint-Victoire cross, from which we can deduce that it was made of two crossing pieces of wood, of equal length, and such that it could be erected in an X shape. If we accept that such was indeed the case we may be committing ourselves to saying that it may have been believed already in the middle of the thirteenth century at Marseilles that St Andrew died on such a special cross. We are not, however, committed to believing that this actual tradition goes any further back, even among the Burgundians.

I was concerned also to find that De la Maduère described a sculpture in the Church of St André de Bâgé (Département de l'Ain), built about 1100, as showing St Andrew 'avec son croix en X'. The carving in question is on the base of a capital, and shows a person crouching in a position of supplication before someone raising a right hand of benediction or absolution. The photographs I have obtained are not very clear, and I suspect the stone is rather worn. This second figure is certainly shown with something in his left hand or over his left shoulder. This has been taken to be a representation of St Andrew, with his cross, but a writer in an authoritative booklet about the church, published in 1988, argues that it is a bishop, who is carrying a crozier. For this writer, and for me, the decisive thing is that the figure has no nimbus (halo); he is not an apostle. (On a capital at the door of the church, Christ, St Peter and three other figures are shown, all with the nimbus.) Here is another alleged early X cross which can be dismissed from consideration!

My investigations into the field of Burgundian history and legend were prompted by the anxiety that in them might lie some important clues to the origin of St Andrew's X-shaped cross. Obviously my research has been limited and superficial, but I think I am entitled to feel reassured so far that there is no evidence here to affect the general conclusions of my argument. I will just add that archaeological evidence for early Burgundian art provides examples of several forms of cross in the Christian context. There is at least one in the shape of an X; this is only to be expected and I doubt if it is significant.

# Part III

## *Accounting for the Cross*

# 11

## *Introductory*

In the preceding chapters I have tried to explain why, on the evidence I have come across so far, I have reached the provisional conclusions that the X-shaped cross of St Andrew was 'invented' in Britain, and that this had happened certainly by the middle of the twelfth century. From that time on, this cross completely dominated the iconographical tradition of the saint in England and Scotland. By the end of the thirteenth century, the idea had spread from Britain to the Continent, and then, more gradually, and less completely, it came to prevail there too.

We could leave the matter there. But I am sure the reader, like myself, is bound to wonder *why* this happened. It may be that in the end we have to say that in the nature of things we cannot expect to get a definitive answer to this question, just as we cannot expect ever to know how the historical St Andrew actually died. However, I do think it is worthwhile to explore some possibilities, and to rule out others. In what follows I intend to develop a few ideas; some perhaps relatively plausible and enticing, others rather more speculative.

As I wrote in an earlier chapter it is commonly claimed, in Scotland at least, that the explanation of the X-shaped cross is that it reflected a belief that Andrew asked to die on a cross different from that of Jesus, being unworthy to be treated as his master had been. The parallel is made with Peter, said to have asked to be crucified head downwards. We have seen that there is absolutely nothing in ancient traditions about St Andrew to give grounds for this story; indeed the emphasis in the *Acta* is on Andrew's devotion to the actual cross of Christ, as physical and symbolic embodiment of the mystery of redemption, and his longing to be accepted by that very cross, to be accepted as worthy to emulate and follow his master by dying in exactly the same way.

It may however be suggested that at some point the Church authorities themselves could have taken up the matter and decided to give St Andrew a special form of martyrdom, to distinguish his death from that of Christ, just as the death of St Peter was distinguished. They then 'invented' the striking (but, as we have seen, somewhat implausible) X shape as the form of Andrew's cross. However, there is no evidence at all for any such debate or decision, no evidence that the adoption of the X-shaped cross was based on a deliberate 'fiat' of the Church, deriving from some theorising of a historical or of a theological kind.

As far as I am aware, there was no serious discussion in the Church, in pre-Reformation times at least, of the significance of the X as being the form of that cross to which St Andrew is supposed to have prayed so movingly, and on which he died. We should also remember that there was no sudden change, over Western Christendom, in the manner in which the saint's death was shown. In Britain, as we have seen, there seem to survive no representations of St Andrew's martyrdom between the Auckland St Andrew cross of about AD 800 (with the saint on a Latin cross) and the Cottam font of about 1140 (with the saint on an X cross); whether in fact there was any 'overlap' between the two forms we cannot therefore say. But on the Continent there is much more evidence, and the adoption of the X cross can be shown to have been gradual and patchy. It would be hard to maintain that there was any attempt to enforce it for some doctrinal reason.

It might still be argued that a 'theoretical' case for giving St Andrew a special cross might have originated, not, as it were, from Rome itself, but from some important religious site or order in Western Europe, and that this inspired certain local painters or sculptors to show his death on the X cross. Other churches and artists would have taken up this idea, and with it the chance, the attractive incentive, to differentiate Andrew's death from that of other apostles. I shall refer again later to this suggestion, when I explore further the possible context in which the adoption of the X cross may be placed.

If we set aside this idea, which is so far unsubstantiated speculation, we have to return to the negative conclusions I have outlined already. The X cross cannot be shown to be derived from the supposed choice of a special cross by a historical Andrew in a historical situation. Nor can it be shown to be derived from a serious doctrinal choice, to have behind its adoption a degree of reasoning and conscious determination.

We have therefore to move on from this type of rationalising explanation and consider other ways in which the X cross may have come into the Andrew iconography. It may be disconcerting even to put forward the idea that the whole thing was due to a 'mistake' or 'accident' of some kind, but there are possibilities here to be explored.

In earlier chapters I have in fact hinted at, or plainly stated, possible explanations for the adoption of the X cross. Was an established practice in Eastern Christendom of showing the saint dying on a tree brought to the West, and then developed or misinterpreted, the tree turning into an X-shaped cross? Was there some confusion with St Vincent, or another saint, portrayed on an 'eculeus' but this thought of as a cross of crucifixion? I do not think there is more to be usefully said about these possibilities, though possibilities they should remain.

Another line of investigation will lead us to look at signs and objects associated with St Andrew and his iconography, and to consider whether they could have been misinterpreted as symbols of a cross of crucifixion, or of the saint's death on such a cross. Many of these images have often in the past been thought of as themselves dependent on the belief that St Andrew died on an X-shaped cross. But could the development have been the other way round? Did the belief come from a misunderstanding of the images?

I begin with the simple 'X' itself, and then go on to discuss other 'X-like' forms and their meanings, noting as I go along associations with St Andrew and possible explanations of this connection.

# 12

## *Understanding 'X'*

This takes us into difficult and challenging territory. We may start with the observation that, among philosophers and theologians, there is a heavy symbolism about the 'X'. Some iconographers have been tempted to look here (at the 'Christian-cosmological significance' (Réau) of the 'X') for an explanation of the St Andrew tradition, for his cross taking this particular shape, although, not surprisingly, they do not venture far into the implications of this abstract scholarly argument.

Now a little reflection will remind us what a tricky symbol the 'X' is. It is an easy and natural form to use in any idle doodling or any conscious designing context, an obvious structure to divide up or decorate a space. Not every X 'means' something! However, in our own culture the 'X' can be used with more purpose – for instance as a sign of approval (on voting papers) or disapproval (against wrong answers in tests). It may signify uncertainty (as in the original designation of the mysterious 'X-rays') or certainty ('X marks the spot'). It can be used as a mathematical symbol of multiplication, or an indication of love (representing kisses at the end of a letter) or of truce ('Pax', with the crossing of two fingers, in a game). For the Romans X, as I have had occasion to mention, meant the number ten, and this is in fact a meaning still understood by most of us today, when we see it in a date or on an old clock face. And that X can mean 'Christ' even in the modern world is obvious from the common abbreviation Xmas for Christmas.

It is easy to appreciate that 'X' could from the early days of the Church have come to stand for 'Christ' since it is the form of the first letter of his name in Greek, the letter we call 'chi'. But in early Christian writing we find comments on the significance of the 'X' that go far beyond this simple point derived from spelling.

The writer on etymology, Isidore, Bishop of Seville from AD 599, explains how the Greeks use letters to represent numbers, but the Romans write out numbers in words, except, he says, for I and X. 'This letter as a shape signifies the cross and as a number means ten.' (*Etym.* 1. 3). Later (*Etym.* 1. 14) he says that the Romans originally used C and S together to represent in writing the sound of the Greek chi (X), and that they only began using the simple X form in the time of Augustus. One manuscript tradition of Isidore's text adds that 'it was the appropriate time for this to happen because X denoted the name of Christ, which was shown by writing this letter, which has the shape of the cross'. Incidentally, if Isidore is thinking of the death of Christ falling in the reign of the Emperor Augustus he is dating it too early, and he is actually wrong about the 'X'. It appears in Latin inscriptions from the second century BC.

In Isidore, however, we do have the X as a letter associated with Christ, and with 'the cross'. (I shall be discussing later what can be meant by saying that X has 'the shape of the cross'.) In an earlier writer, Justin Martyr, who died about AD 165, we find a more complicated story. Justin's *Apology 1* is addressed to the Emperor Antoninus Pius; it is a very interesting work, not least because it is one of the earliest Christian writings not meant primarily for fellow Christians to read, but intended to put a case to the pagan men of power, the men who could be sensible and stop the persecution of Christians. Justin was steeped in classical literature and philosophy, and he attempts to make this serve the Christian cause. For instance he writes of Plato with respect, but as one who learnt from the Jewish prophets and from Moses. In one passage he says that Plato in the dialogue *Timaeus* was enquiring into the nature of the son of God, and 'placed him in the universe in the manner of the letter X' (*Apol.* 1. 60). Later he implies that this was because Plato had misunderstood the account of Moses' actions (in Numbers 21.9), which, Justin says, involved the figure of the cross. Plato took instead the reference to be to the letter form X.

In fact, Justin is not at all a reliable witness to what is written in the Old Testament or to how it should be interpreted. No better is his understanding of Plato! However, the passage in Plato's cosmological work *Timaeus* to which he refers (*Tim.* 36 B-C) has been brought into arguments about the origins and meaning of Christian symbols, both in early and in more recent times, so I cannot ignore it entirely. To give an oversimplified summary of Plato's thought: he is describing how the Creator gave the universe, its body and its soul, a spherical structure, by first dividing its 'matter' into two lengths and then fitting them together, middle to middle ('like a chi' he says), and bending them round upon themselves to make an inner and an outer circle. The mention, specifically, of a 'chi' here seems to me to have been a matter of chance (and not of deep significance!) on Plato's part; it is, however, perhaps understandable that much has been made of it.

The tendency in Christian apologists to find foreshadowings of Christ and his manner of death in earlier writing, in both classical authors and in the Old Testament, is well known. In a previous chapter (see pp. 32–4) I referred to a passage of St Jerome, quoted by Lipsius in his discussion of the 'crux decussata'. In his *Commentary on Jeremiah* (ch. 31). Jerome writes of the story in Genesis where Joseph took his sons Manasseh and Ephraim to be blessed by his father, who was very old and almost blind. Joseph placed Ephraim on his right towards Jacob's left hand and Manasseh on his left towards Jacob's right hand. But Jacob 'reached out his right hand and put it on Ephraim's head, though he was the younger, and, crossing his arms, he put his left hand on Manasseh's head, even though Manasseh was the firstborn'. Joseph tried to correct this 'mistake' but Jacob insisted that his blessing was intentional, and that the younger brother would be greater than the elder. Jerome uses the phrase 'in mysterio crucis decussatis manibus' to describe Jacob's action – his hands formed an X shape as a symbol of the cross.

This concept was not original to Jerome; it appears already in, for example, Tertullian, and it proved a popular and lasting Christian interpretation of the significance of the story. We do have to recognise in material such as this that 'the cross' is to be understood symbolically, not literally. The X shape is not supposed to be the form of the actual cross on which Christ died. It is *like* that form in that it is made from two crossing lines, and it is represented in early Christian iconography as right-angled. It is very similar in fact to the 'Greek' cross, also right-angled and equal-armed, but set upright (✚), and to be similarly understood, not as Christ's actual cross of crucifixion but as a symbol of that death and of Christianity itself. In the case of the X cross, of course, there was the additional weight of 'meaning', in that, as we have seen, it had the form of the chi, the initial letter of the name of Christ.

In addition to all the evidence from early Christian art of the widespread use of both these forms of cross, there is written evidence from medieval times of a lasting appreciation of the symbolism of the 'X'. The first book of the *Rationale Divinorum Officiorum* by Durandus, Bishop of Mende in France in the last part of the thirteenth century, deals with the symbolism to be found (and to be employed) in the architecture and furnishing of churches. (This is symbolism carried to extremes; circular stairs signify the hidden knowledge of the Church, and so on.) Durandus describes in detail the manner in which the dedication of a church must be carried out. Twelve crosses are to be depicted on the walls inside the church, and twelve lamps are to burn before them. (I shall write something about dedication crosses later.) The bishop is to enter the church, and on its pavement a cross has to be made of ashes and sand. On this cross the bishop is to scratch with his staff the letters of the Greek alphabet one way and the Latin alphabet the other. Durandus says that this represents the union in faith of the two peoples, the Jews and the Greeks 'which is made through the Cross of Christ; according to the saying that Jacob blessed his sons with his hands crossed' (*RDO* 1. 21–2). The detailed description makes it clear that the cross is to run from the *corners* of the church pavement, that is, in an X shape (whether right-angled, or perhaps elongated).

All this evidence shows the importance of the X shape in Christian writing and in Christian art. In this relatively early material we should note that there are no references to St

Andrew. The 'X' symbolism was a persistent element in thinking in the West, however, and that at a later date it *could* be
brought into association with St Andrew was shown in an
earlier chapter when I wrote about Lipsius and his treatment of
the 'crux decussata'.

Before getting back to St Andrew and his particular iconography I shall end this rather abstract discussion with a
mention of *The Garden of Cyrus*, by Sir Thomas Browne, published in 1658, which nicely brings together much of what I
have been discussing. This short work is devoted to the 'quincunx', a pattern commonly used in the planting, especially of
fruit trees (like the pattern of the five on dice). In his final
chapter, where he is writing of the mystical significance of the X
shape, and of the number five, both characteristic of the
'quincunx', Browne does refer to the passage in Plato's *Timaeus*.
However in his first chapter, although he refers to 'decussation',
which he says has the form of 'an Andrean or Burgundian
cross', he rejects comparison of the 'quincunx' with forms of the
cross. He writes: 'We shall decline [i.e. not discuss] the old
theme, so traced by antiquity, of crosses and crucifixion.' He
does in fact go on briefly to discuss different forms of cross,
ending with 'the cross of our blessed Saviour'. And 'since the
learned Lipsius hath made some doubt even of the cross of St
Andrew' this too is not to be taken as relevant to the interpretation and history of the 'quincunx'.

However, as I have shown, there are X shapes written of and
used in Christian contexts to which a symbolic significance was
certainly attached. Now, there are various examples of an 'X'
actually associated with St Andrew in the iconographic record.
Can we give these 'X's a meaning? Or is there anything in this
material that is likely to have given rise to the idea that the saint
died on an actual cross of this form? We need to be careful,
perhaps a bit sceptical too. There has been a natural tendency
to try to make significant any apparent use of the 'X' in
connection with St Andrew.

In Trier there is a reliquary casket dating from the time of
Archbishop Egbert (AD 977–93) and associated with St Andrew. The border decoration on the sides contains various

motifs, including some X patterns, and on one end of the casket are two large X shapes made from pearls. It is going too far, in my view, to claim that these must have been meant to symbolise St Andrew's cross of crucifixion, and that the casket can be used to prove that the idea that the saint died on an X-shaped cross was indeed current in some quarters by AD 1000. (It is another question whether these shapes could at some later date have been mistakenly understood as having some reference to his martyrdom.) It is possible that the X forms or crosses here were meant as deliberate *Christian* symbols. It is also surely possible that they were purely decorative (plate 18).*

There are two striking representations of St Andrew that show him on an upright cross but include apparent X shapes. In Besse-en-Chandesse, near Clermont-Ferrand in France, there is a Church of St Andrew, the core of which dates from the twelfth century. A capital there shows St Andrew's martyrdom. The identification is certain because on the capital there is an inscription referring to the 'Passio' of 'Andrew the Apostle'. The saint is shown on an upright cross with a figure each side (angels rather than executioners). Andrew is fastened to this cross with ropes that bind his feet together on the upright and his wrists to the two arms of the cross. The ropes are tied in such a way as to make three very prominent X shapes.†

These ropes at Besse have caught the attention of some iconographers. Réau writes 'We know how often misunderstood images give rise to legends' and he says 'Perhaps the crossing ropes gave artists the idea of representing the saint as tied to a cross of diagonal beams'. I do not myself find this at all a plausible suggestion, and would favour above it an explanation based on misinterpretation of such X or X-like symbols associated with St Andrew as I discuss in the two following chapters. I wonder in fact if the Xs here, with Andrew indisputably on an upright cross, were meant by the artist to reinforce the *Christian* symbolism of the piece, and to encourage the notion that St Andrew had a very special devotion to the Church as so symbolised? I doubt very much whether they can have had anything to do with engendering the idea that St Andrew died on an X-shaped cross.

26. Martyrdom of St Andrew, capital of *c*.1200, in Church of S. André, Besse-en-Chandesse, France (Photo: P. Nuger)

27. Reconstructed cross at Auckland St Andrew. For detail, see Fig. 14 (Photo: courtesy of St Andrew with St Anne PCC)

I come to the same conclusion about the British example to which I referred briefly in a previous chapter: the shaft of a cross at Auckland St Andrew. (This too has been used by a recent iconographer (Calvert) in support of the view that the origin of the X cross idea is perhaps to be found in such an image.) Here we have a man on an upright cross with ropes fastening him to it across his chest – his arms are not visible and are to be supposed to be somehow behind the two parts of the cross beam. This particular detail has parallels. There are many examples of illustrations of Christ's crucifixion where the two *thieves* are shown with their arms behind the cross bar, usually, I think, with the letters of their names written on the two exposed pieces of wood each side. An early Spanish manuscript, the Beatus *Commentaries on the Apocalypse* in Gerona, has such a scene, and a painting of about 1464 by Justus van Gent, in Ghent's St Bavon Cathedral, also shows the two thieves with their arms hanging behind the bar of their crosses.

The ropes used in the British case to tie the figure to the cross round the chest form a decided X. This feature too is certainly to be found in other representations of crucifixions. There are examples of Christ himself being so depicted, and I have read that this is a Syrian motif. One instance, in the Hermitage Museum in St Petersburg, is a silver plate of the sixth or seventh century with an inscription in Syriac. This has an engraving of the crucifixion of Christ and the two thieves. All three are shown tied to upright crosses with 'X' ropes across their chests. Is the use of the device simply freakish in such cases, or, as I have wondered, did it have the significance that we have seen could be attached to the X as a symbol of Christian faith?

The Auckland cross shaft seems to fit into a group of standing crosses of around AD 800 in northern England, which had figures of all, or several, of the apostles round the base and/ or on the sides. This has been described as a British development, which made use of the local tradition of these great crosses – thought to have stood in the open – to present and popularise the apostles, so often shown on the Continent in mosaic and painting, but inside the churches.

Here, in addition to other figures, probably apostles, we have one given special prominence, and it is generally accepted that the saint is meant to be St Andrew (to whom the church where the cross now is is dedicated). On the upright above his head there seem to be the letters PAS (for passio), and on the left side of the cross bar as we look at it there are the letters AND. The right side is lost so we have not got the complete name. Accepting that this is St Andrew we may ask why did the sculptor show him in this way? Was it the artist's own, or a locally inspired, idea, or was he following a model? One suggestion that has been made is that there was here a deliberate attempt to depart from what was by then the usual way of showing the crucifixion of Christ, which might have seemed inappropriate for a mere apostle. The sculptor found another model in depictions known to him of the crucifixion of the thieves, with their arms behind the cross bar, and used that (with the crossing ropes to indicate how a victim in this position might have been fastened to the cross). I do not find this a convincing explanation, and I feel I must leave open the question of where this portrayal came from. But I do not think it can have derived from any theory about St Andrew dying on an X-shaped cross, or, indeed, that in itself it can have led to such a theory.

Other relatively early X shapes are the 'saltires' found in heraldry. They do appear on shields in coats of arms from 1150 or so, and some famous Scottish families, including the Bruces, had such devices. Some personal seals from the mid thirteenth century show shields with such saltires. However, I do not think there is any evidence to suggest that these early saltires had special reference to St Andrew; they were one form in which the 'cross of Christ' could be shown, as the badge of those fighting for the faith against the infidel. There are saltires too on the shields of some of the famous Lewis chessmen, the walrus-ivory figures dating from the mid twelfth century, but it is disputed whether these should be seen as heraldic, or merely decorative or even structural devices.

I shall be discussing later the apparent saltires on what were ecclesiastical seals definitely associated with St Andrew, and what they might have meant.

In the course of this study so far we have explored, and rejected, the idea that some simple X shapes found associated with images of St Andrew might have been misunderstood or have given rise to the idea that the saint was put to death on a cross of this shape. But in the following chapters we need to look further at other possible explanations that follow this general line of argument: that the origin of the idea in Britain was some misinterpretation of an artistic tradition about St Andrew, or of some religious belief or practice reflected in art, which came to influence his iconography. I should perhaps warn the reader that, having started with the hope that something like a plausible theory might be constructed from these considerations, I have not been able to satisfy myself that anything more can be found than possibilities, with very little to support them. Perhaps there are arguments or evidence that I have missed.

# Notes

\* (p. 135)   My reluctance to accept the Trier casket as providing evidence for a tradition alive already in AD 1000 that St Andrew died on an X-shaped cross stems from this early date. With the Autun troper taken out of the argument there is nothing which is comparable, nothing so far found which is earlier than the twelfth century. There certainly is no doubt of the association of the Trier casket with St Andrew. The only alteration to it after its original making seems to have been the addition of the feet of crouching lions. Apparently it functioned right from the start both as reliquary and portable altar. On the top, in the space before the foot, there is inserted a small altar-stone with the inscription which says it was consecrated in honour of St Andrew. Round the outside of the top is another inscription, which says that Archbishop Egbert ordered the making of the casket, and decided that it should hold holy relics, including a nail from Christ's death on the cross, a tooth of St Peter, with some of his beard and part of his chains, and a sandal of St Andrew. These two inscriptions are judged contemporary, dating, with the casket itself, to Archbishop Egbert's time, before AD 1000. It is interesting that the casket did contain other relics, beside 'St Andrew's sandal'. I suppose it may have been the fact that the sandal was the most substantial thing, and something that could be represented as a 'speaking relic' (represented as like itself), which led to the foot and sandal being made and placed on the top and to the consecration of the altar in honour of St Andrew (rather than St Peter?).

† (p. 135)   A note in the church guide suggests that a date before 1205 for this capital can be inferred from the fact that St Andrew is shown on an upright cross: 'from 1205, the date of the 4th crusade, the cross of St Andrew had the form of an X'. I hope I have shown that such a statement, made in the context of French iconography, can hardly be justified. A reference to the crusade does, however, make some sense, since it seems that from about this date crosses of various kinds, including 'saltires', came to be used on shields and banners, a practice playing its part in the development of the whole art of heraldry. As I write in my text I think in origin this had nothing to do with St Andrew.

# 13

## *'X' as the Cross*

I have several times already referred to the fact that in Christian iconography an X shape could be interpreted as 'a cross' in the sense of a symbol of Christianity, of Christ and the faith, and such simple forms of the cross turn up, especially as inscribed in casual, often archaeological, contexts.

We have also seen that there was a close link in the written tradition between St Andrew and 'the cross', and we may start by considering early iconographic material from the Continent which certainly represents the saint, not *on*, but *with* a cross, whether realistically portrayed or symbolic, and see what shape this cross is given, and how we may best explain it. We shall then look at the British evidence, and the examples where St Andrew is shown with some form of cross, and in particular those cases where he is associated with the special X shape, or something that could be understood as such. What is the meaning of such crosses? Are they all to be interpreted as dependent on the idea that the saint died on such a cross, an idea therefore already established and determining the saint's iconography in Britain? Or are they a possible source for a mistaken idea that he did?

In an earlier chapter I referred to some examples reproduced in Rohault of early portrayals of the death of St Andrew on an upright cross (see p. 49 and fig. 8, p. 50). In one an illuminated initial in a manuscript of the ninth century is made up of two scenes: St Andrew hanging on such a cross, and St Andrew being led to the cross, making his famous address to it, with a crowd listening. The cross is shown in both cases as plain, with the three visible extremities apparently slightly enlarged (in a decorative rather than a realistic way?). An enamel triptych of the twelfth century from Trier, which I mentioned in an earlier chapter (see fig. 3, p. 23), has a scene of angels at the tomb of St Andrew, a scene of the saint tied to the upright cross (the ropes, incidentally, forming three X shapes round his wrists and his feet), and a scene of Andrew kneeling by the cross and praying to it. The cross here is large and very plain, as if simply made from two planks of wood. In these cases we have a direct representational reference to the passion story of the saint, and awareness of the importance of his address to the cross.

A thirteenth-century enamel has a figure named as Andrew, seated, and holding in one hand a model of a church and in the other a very plain medium-sized Latin cross. A twelfth-century manuscript has the saint, named here too, seated and holding a Latin cross, with its beams rather wider at their ends than in the centre. In spite of the elaboration in this case I think these crosses should probably be interpreted not as symbols of the saint's devotion to 'the cross' but explicitly as symbols of his actual martyrdom, here understood as being on the Latin cross. I wrote in an earlier chapter of the evidence from French and German cathedrals – evidence for the apostles being shown with their instruments of martyrdom – and of St Andrew being shown first with a Latin cross, and later with an X-shaped one.

Another feature of the iconography of St Andrew, however, is the practice of showing him with a long staff surmounted by an equal-armed 'Greek' cross, usually with elaborated ends. There are several examples, for instance in early mosaics, where he is the only one of a row of apostles shown with this attribute, and I do believe this must be meant as a symbolic recognition of his special devotion to 'the cross'. A good example in sculpture is in the cloister at Moissac, Tarn-et-Garonne, France, completed in 1100. The four corner piers carry almost life-size figures of eight apostles, carved in shallow relief with their names above them. Peter is carrying keys, some of the others have scrolls or books. None has an attribute relating to his death. Andrew alone has a long staff topped by a cross. A commentator implies that this way of representing Andrew is not unusual.

An example showing St Peter with keys and St Andrew with cross-topped staff is in a twelfth century wall painting now in the Museum of Catalan Art in Barcelona (plate 20), and I referred in an earlier chapter to an altar frontal there on which St Andrew is distinguished from other apostles by being shown carrying such a staff. A troper from Britain, now held in the British Library, and dating from the third quarter of the eleventh century has an illumination with a figure seated and holding a long staff with cross in his right hand. The figure is named as 'pater Andreas'.

Could such a use of a staff with the 'Greek' cross, in association with St Andrew, and perhaps on occasion shown on a slant so that it resembled an X, have led to its identification as a symbol, not of his devotion to the cross, but of his execution on a cross of special shape?

I have already mentioned examples of St Andrew being shown holding in front of him a small cross – as in the thirteenth-century sculpture in Worcester Cathedral. For a while I was inclined to interpret such crosses as intended as symbols of his devotion to 'the cross'. I wondered whether they could later have been misunderstood as symbols of his martyrdom and, because of the angle at which these crosses are usually held, have led to the idea that the saint died on an X-shaped cross.

However, I now believe that the possibility that small crosses of apparent X shape held by the saint should be understood as symbolic, not of 'the cross' but of his actual *crucifixion*, has to be allowed for much earlier than I had thought likely.

Crosses of this kind seem to appear in the iconography alongside examples of St Andrew actually shown *on* his cross, as we saw particularly in the case of English embroidery (although there is nothing to match the exceptionally early representation apparently showing our saint on the X-cross on the Cottam font). Also, I am impressed by the fact that there is a consistency in the way these crosses are portrayed, at least in the British examples. They are plain, they are usually thin, they are unlike those crosses, whether Latin or Greek, which are meant as symbols of faith, of the Church. These latter crosses usually, where there is any pretension at all to art, have some elaboration of shape or of decoration. I would now classify any thin, simple, straight-ended X-cross associated with St Andrew as meant as a symbol of his death, and thus derivative from an established belief that he died on such a cross, rather than likely in itself to have given rise to such a belief.

It remains true that in early Christian art in Britain there are to be found crosses of several shapes and degrees of sophistication which were symbolic of faith and the Church, and so not meant as representational crosses of crucifixion. Among these are found a few of a simple X shape. For example, there are 'saltires' on the shaft of a standing cross from the island of Inchmarnock, off Bute. Could it be that such a cross or crosses, if used in a context associated with St Andrew, might have been misinterpreted as representing his cross of martyrdom?

A particular use of cross symbols, which I have already had occasion to refer to, was in the dedication, or rather the consecration, of churches. Surviving symbols of this type are to be found on the exterior, and/or the interior, walls of many early churches in Britain. (An especially good set is to be seen in Salisbury Cathedral.) Early examples of the Norman period include incised upright crosses, of Latin or of Greek style, but there are also from before 1200 examples of what became the commonest form, the four-petal shape (or the 'cross–of-arcs'

28. St Andrew, with St Peter and St James, on tomb of 1501 at Jerpoint Abbey, Co. Kilrenny, Eire. Note the thin plain cross (Photo: Leslie Reid)

shape) within a circle. There are surviving parts of two very large such crosses on the external walls of the ruins of St Andrews Cathedral, and a smaller one can be clearly seen on a western wall of the church in nearby Crail. This type of cross has a superficial likeness to an X shape, but I do not think it could possibly have been misinterpreted anywhere as representing a cross of crucifixion.

29. Dedication cross, of 1243, at Crail Parish Church, Fife (Photo: U. Hall)

There is however one piece of evidence concerning church dedication which is of especial interest. This is an inscription that actually records the foundation of the Church of St Paul at Jarrow in Northumbria in AD 685 (which Bede will have witnessed as a boy of twelve). The inscription is prefaced by a small chi-rho sign, in its original Roman form. In other cases in Anglo-Saxon England, such as at Deerhurst, dedicatory inscriptions are prefaced by a simple equal-armed 'Greek' cross. The Jarrow case seems to be unique, and it is probably to be accounted for by the close link with 'Roman' church traditions in Northumbria.

30. (Part of) dedication inscription at Church of St Paul, Jarrow, of AD 685. Note the chi-rho (Photo: T. Middlemass. © Corpus of Anglo-Saxon Stone Sculpture, University of Durham)

Now it will be recalled that it was from Jarrow that King Nechtan of the Picts requested builders for a church of St Peter in his own land in AD 710. Would a dedicatory stone there have had the chi-rho symbol, as at Jarrow? Would a church of St Andrew in Pictland founded perhaps only a generation later, probably also under Northumbrian influence, have had this symbol too? Was there scope here for misinterpretation?

# 14

## *The Chi-Rho*

I have already had occasion to refer to and describe the symbol of the chi-rho, the 'monogram' of the name of Christ. We saw that the Rohault authors found a resemblance to it in the figure in the Autun troper, which they mistakenly identified as St Andrew. We saw that the vision said to have inspired the Emperor Constantine in AD 312 is usually interpreted as a vision of the chi-rho, and I have suggested that it is this story which lies behind the St Andrews legend of King Angus.

Is there any evidence that a chi-rho figure was ever misunderstood as a depiction of a man being crucified on an X-shaped cross? Could it be that such a figure, used in the context of the cult of St Andrew, was misunderstood as representing the death of this saint?

It has been tempting for iconographers to float this idea, but for it to be taken seriously I think we have to go into more detail and consider the 'how' and the 'when' involved in such a misunderstanding.

There are plenty of examples of the chi-rho in a relatively simple form from the early centuries of the Christian Church. It is found from the third century – along with examples of the iota-chi, which is a similar monogram, formed from IX, 'Iesus Christus'. Originally such compound letter forms were no more than space-saving devices, and it is interesting that even the chi-rho has been found in non-Christian contexts acting as an acceptable abbreviation of a quite different word. In the Christian context, in the catacombs and elsewhere, the use of the chi-rho was surely mainly precautionary, designed to conceal meaning from all but those already initiated into the Christian community.

From the time of Constantine the chi-rho appears much more commonly and openly. It formed part of the battle standard, or 'labarum' of the emperor, and as such is reproduced on coins of the time (See fig. 16, p. 96). As a symbol it came to be usually represented within a circle, interpreted as an indication of God's rule over the whole world, and within the device were frequently included an A and a Ω or ω, 'alpha' and 'omega', the first and last letters of the Greek alphabet, also symbolising the completeness of God's rule.

A literary description of the chi-rho is to be found in the poet Paulinus, writing in the early fifth century. He describes a precious possession of his church at Nola in southern Italy, which incorporated two forms of 'cross'. One had the appearance of a ship's mast with a single upright and a cross piece. The other 'had a second shape, and told of the Lord Christ by a kind of monogram'. Paulinus then describes the chi-rho (though he manages to find in it all six Greek letters representing XRISTO! [Paul, Poem 19]). It is interesting that he calls this device too a 'cross' ('crux'), obviously meaning by this the cross as the most important symbol of Christian faith.

A well-known and often reproduced chi-rho is that shown on a shield held by guards of the Emperor Justinian in the mosaic depicting him with his retinue in the Church of San Vitale in Ravenna. This dates from AD 547. It may have been designed as a conscious copy of the chi-rho used by Constantine (plate 19). Certainly by this time such a simple and obviously 'monogrammatic' form was going out of fashion, and we find examples where the X has been turned into an upright, 'Greek', cross, and the P (the 'rho') has been incorporated into it, forming just a modification of the upright stroke. Good examples of the two forms of chi-rho are to be seen on the sixth-century tomb of Archbishop Theodorus, in the Church of Sant'Apollinare in Classe, Ravenna.* Both forms remained powerful and recognisable *Christian* symbols; how far they were still understood as having direct reference to the *name* of Christ I suppose is doubtful.

If we look for chi-rhos in the British material we do find a few examples of the simple 'Constantinian' type, the one which does look a bit like a man on an X cross. Examples from the time of

31. The seventh-century tomb of Archbishop Theodore, in Sant'Apollinare in Classe, Ravenna, showing two forms of chi-rho (The Bridgeman Art Library, London)

the Roman occupation are a cup with this motif placed six times around the rim, and a painting on wall plaster at Lullingstone Villa in Kent. There have been found in Britain coins of late Roman usurpers which use the device of the Constantinian 'labarum'.†

A later example of the early form of chi-rho in northern Britain is the one I have already described, that in the dedication inscription at St Paul's, Jarrow (see fig. 30, p. 146). This dates from AD 685, and attention has been drawn by commentators to the fact that it has this 'Roman' form, which of course is consistent with the other evidence for the close links between the Church in Northumbria and the authorities in Rome.

However, alongside this we have to set early examples of the developed form I described above. At Kirkmadrine on the Rhins peninsula in Galloway there are three large pillar stones thought to date from the fifth century. One has on it an upright cross, in a circle, with the rho-figure developed into a hooked or crooked shape, which, as I have said, came to be a frequent form of the symbol.) Beneath are the Latin words 'initium et finis' = 'the beginning and the end'. Another stone has a similar 'chi-rho' with the hooked feature, incised within a circle, and with an alpha and an omega ( = 'the beginning and the end') placed above it. Below the chi-rho there is a Latin inscription saying that two bishops are buried here.

A somewhat later stone at Whithorn (the 'Peter Stone') has

32. Fifth-century stones from Kirkmadrine, Galloway, showing forms of chi-rho (From: Stuart, *The Sculptured Stones of Scotland*, vol. 2)

33. Stone at Whithorn, with reference to St Peter and form of chi-rho (From: Stuart, *The Sculptured Stones of Scotland*, vol. 2)

what is called a 'cross-of-arcs' within a double circle, and the upper arm of this cross has attached to it what must be seen as a 'rho' figure – or a figure derived from that symbol. An upright slab at Raasay, Skye, has a similar device incised on it. And to be particularly noted is a stone (the 'Skeith Stone')at Kilrenny, Fife not far from St Andrews. This has on it a more elaborate 'cross-of-arcs', and here too some investigators have seen an apparent 'rho' in the design.

We are considering the possibility that a misunderstanding of a chi-rho figure could have led to the idea of crucifixion on an X-shaped cross. I asked at the beginning of this chapter if there is evidence that this misunderstanding ever took place. I have to say that I have not come across any such evidence, as a general idea about crucifixion, or as a provable development in the iconography of any individual saint. What about the more specific claim that this was how the idea of St Andrew's death originated? Could it have happened in this way, in Britain?

I think it is reasonable to suggest that for this to have been the case, there would have had to be one or more such chi-rho figures locally available for misinterpretation, but not such a common use of the symbol as to make misunderstanding unlikely. Now clearly the developed form of the chi-rho could not have been responsible, as the most notable thing about it is that it has lost the X shape altogether. But how familiar remained the earlier form, which is the one that might be misunderstood?

We come back to two relevant things: first, the legend of King Angus and its likely dependence on the Constantine story of the vision of the chi-rho, which might have led to some representation of that symbol at St Andrews, not understood later; and secondly the dedication at Jarrow and the possibility that a chi-rho figure used in the consecration of a church of St Andrew among the Picts might, a few generations afterwards, have been interpreted as showing the martyrdom of that saint on an X-shaped cross.

Several cogent objections can be made to these versions of the theory, not least that they require tying the 'invention' of the X-cross to St Andrews itself, which has its problems. I shall give weight to them in a later chapter. Let me leave it here as the faintest of possibilities!

## Notes

\* (p. 148)   Is it puzzling that both forms are used on the same monument? (To me the first impression of the second device here is that in itself it suggests, not a chi-rho, but a Greek cross modified to incorporate a bishop's crozier!) What explanation is given by iconographers of the development of the later form of chi-rho? Is it adequately accounted for by the 'tendency to graphic simplification' (as e.g. Thomas)? I remain rather puzzled by it all. I certainly agree with Thomas that for the 'majority of Western' Christians the device must have been 'no more than a symbol; it would not have been perceived as containing actual and separable letters'.

† (p. 149)   An interesting Romano-British chi-rho is that depicted in a mosaic found at Hinton St Mary, where the device is shown behind the head of the figure usually interpreted as Christ. Professor George Henderson has referred me to a comparable image at Naples – St Januarius with a chi-rho rather than a nimbus behind his head. Could a similar image of St Andrew, which thus showed his association with an X-shape, have been misinterpreted as relating to death on a special shape of cross? This suggestion seems to me no more fanciful than the theory I discussed in an earlier chapter, derived from images of the saint shown with ropes forming an X across his chest.

# 15

# *The 'Saltires' on Seals*

I have already had occasion to mention that some early ecclesiastical seals show symbols that have been interpreted as saltires, that is, as representations of an X-shaped cross of crucifixion, the cross on which St Andrew is supposed to have died. The matter deserves some further discussion.

We have seen that in other media, such as embroidery and wall painting, there are early examples of the saint shown on his X-shaped cross, and there are examples that are not much later than these, or are even contemporaneous with them, where St Andrew is shown carrying a small symbolic X-shaped cross. But what about examples of an 'X' on its own, without the saint, but used in a context where it must have been understood as evoking the particular cross of St Andrew? I do not think certain examples of such an image appear, in artefacts or in literary reference, before the fourteenth century, and they then occur, not primarily in religious material, but rather with political meaning, on flags and banners, on coins, and on soldiers' battle-dress, where they have reference to Scottish identity.

We saw that there are a number of seals, from different places in Britain and dating from the thirteenth century, which show St Andrew actually on an X-shaped cross. Several types with this device are to be associated with St Andrews itself, its church and clergy. There are also a few examples from the thirteenth century (none, I think, from St Andrews) showing the saint carrying a cross of X shape. A very worn seal of Robert de Berkeley, Sub-Dean of Wells, shows St Andrew seated, holding what appears to be a small X cross. This is dated really early – to 1230. A large seal of Peterborough shows a boat on waves (a symbol of the Church), with three saints standing in it,

34. Thirteenth-century seal of Peterborough Cathedral, showing St Andrew, St Paul and St Peter (From Pedrick, *Monastic Seals of the Thirteenth Century*)

under architectural canopies. St Paul is in the centre, holding a sword, St Peter to the right, with keys and a book, and St Andrew to the left, holding a small plain X cross. What is particularly interesting is that the inscription on the seal refers to the three symbols – the cross, the keys and the sword (crux, claves, ensis). We are reminded of St Andrew's special association with 'the cross', and of the Rochester seal which has on it the legend 'I am the servant of the cross of Christ' (see fig. 21, p. 103). So, could the cross – the 'crux' – depicted and actually referred to on the Peterborough seal symbolise the cross of Christ to which Andrew showed devotion, or is it meant as the cross of his own crucifixion? I tend to think the latter, judging from its form and the way it is held.

However, I do not know of any thirteenth or even fourteenth-century seals that restrict their reference to St Andrew to the image of an X – except for the very seals that I have now to discuss! It does seem to me unlikely that the church authorities would have used such an image, intending it to be understood as a cross of crucifixion, before ever people became familiar with the portrayal of the saint actually on such a cross on their seals.

What are we to make, therefore, of the apparent 'saltires'
on seals of 1200 or earlier?

The seals in question are
those used by St Andrews Priory, and a few associated with
the Diocese of Bath and Wells.
(There may be others, from
other places, to which my attention has not so far been
drawn.) The St Andrews examples that are available for us
to study, actual seals, matrices
and replicas, cover a number
of centuries. I described earlier
the main elements that stay
constant while other details
change (see p. 104). The seals
show a church with tower, and
in the field either side of the
tower an equal-armed 'Greek'

35. Replica of third seal of
St Andrews Cathedral Chapter.
St Andrews Cathedral Museum (©
Crown copyright, reproduced cour-
tesy of Historic Scotland)

cross shape and an apparent 'saltire' X shape. The seals are of
course frequently rather worn and the details indistinct. However I think it can be said with certainty that the 'Greek' cross is
just that, a representation of 'the cross' as symbol of the Christian
faith. This cross is shown with an elaboration of the four points
(cf. the heraldic 'cross potent' and 'cross flory'). It is also certain
that in the best preserved examples the X shape also has the four
extremities developed or extended. The ends are not cut off
sharply at right angles.

In writing about artistic representations of the execution
cross of St Andrew in symbolic form, whether as a large object
associated with the saint, or as a small cross which he carries, I
claimed that it always appears as a plain structure, as if made
from two planks or laths, without elaborated ends. (There are
other cases, of course, where the cross is shown as made of rough
tree trunks or branches, but these are not relevant to our
argument.) The way in which the X is shown on the seals is

different and this suggests that it is not meant to symbolise the saint's cross of crucifixion.*

What did it symbolise, then? One attractive idea is that it too, with its developed extremities, simply symbolised 'the cross', the cross, that is, as emblem of Christianity. We have seen that the 'X' could certainly be so understood, and there are numerous examples in Christian art and archaeology where this meaning is clear.

Should we carry the argument further? It might be claimed that any symbols of the cross would have been particularly appropriate where St Andrew was the saint in whose name the church was dedicated, because of the importance of devotion to 'the cross' in his own traditional story. I did suggest earlier that the cross in the special X form might have come to be associated with him in iconography at an early date, simply for this reason. However, this is no more than speculation. As far as our seals go, I would prefer to leave it as a possibility that the ✛ and the X both represented 'the cross' as symbol of faith and the Church. The next question of course would be, was the X here, on seals produced at St Andrews, *subsequently* given the different Andrew connection by being reinterpreted as an unusual cross of crucifixion, special to this saint?

There is another possibility. My attention was first drawn to the problem of these seals by a sharp-eyed friend, who, on seeing a number of seal replicas in the Cathedral Museum at St Andrews, said that the X-shaped device on them looked like 'crossed bones'. On several of these seals indeed it does. The extremities of the X show knobbly 'blobs', features that are characteristic of the long bones of human arms and legs. It is noteworthy that it is on some of the later seals of this type that the similarity to bones is most marked; seals that were produced long after the saltire shape, the X cross, was indisputably associated with St Andrew and his death on such a cross.

Now we have become familiar with the device of 'crossed bones' on tombstones and in other religious contexts, but my research so far has failed to find examples of this image going back into the early Middle Ages. It is therefore admittedly strange if it was actually used on seals from the end of the twelfth century.

And why should such a device have been used? I have written above of the legend of the bringing of relics to St Andrews, and have accepted that there were actual bones (however obtained) to be revered in the great cathedral. The reliquary was supposed to contain a kneecap, a tooth and finger bones, and an arm bone. It was of course of enormous significance that the church at St Andrews could claim to have actual corporeal relics of the apostle. Is it plausible to suppose that it could have advertised this fact on the priory seals? But why should the device show two long bones, crossed in the X shape – unless this was already recognised as a way in which to show the presence of bone relics?

36. Seal of Bishop Burnel, Bath and Wells, 1275–92. British Library, seal Add.ch. 20287 (By permission of the British Library)

The seals of Bath and Wells need to be considered too. The church at Wells is an ancient St Andrew dedication, and must have had relics of some kind, but there is no tradition of there being actual bones of the saint there. There is a fine thirteenth-century seal of the Dean and Chapter (of Wells, apparently), which has the image of St Andrew on his X-shaped cross. Also, several seals survive which are to be attributed to Robert Burnel, Bishop of Bath and Wells from 1275 to 1292. These show the bishop, full length, with his right hand raised in benediction, and a crozier in his left hand. In the field are what are described as 'the emblems of St Peter and St Andrew': on the left of the seal are keys, and on the right is a thin X shape, slightly elongated rather than right-angled in form.

At this date, of course, the allusion might have been meant to be to St Andrew's cross of crucifixion, although, as I have said, there do not seem to be other thirteenth- or fourteenth-century

examples of this simple symbolic use on seals. A clear photograph of one of these seals seems to me to show definite
development of the ends of the X, as on the somewhat earlier
St Andrews seals. I have to say, however, that the feature here
certainly looks more like a triple-headed decorative elaboration
than like the ends of bones! The device might therefore here be
deliberately designed to represent the 'cross of faith'. Or was it
an image simply taken over from, or adapted from, some other
source or centre – even from St Andrews itself?

Now I do not want to push this speculation too far. But we
are perhaps tempted to ask whether it could have been the X
shape shown on early priory seals at St Andrews (however we
interpret this shape and account for it) that led to the idea that
St Andrew died on an X-shaped cross. I shall take up shortly
the difficulties in this apparently straightforward suggestion; for
now I may just remind the reader that the figure on the Cottam
font dates from fifty or so years earlier than the earliest of these
Scottish seals!

## Note

* (p. 156)   There are sixteenth-century seals associated with St
   Andrews (e.g. one of the 'Official of Lothian' dated 1543), which
   show the saint holding in front of him a large X cross, with straight
   ends to its arms, together with two small X crosses, in the field each
   side of him, which show distinctly expanded, 'lumpy', ends. What
   significance did they have?

# 16

## *The Cross in Context*

We have now considered a number of possible explanations for the adoption of the X-shaped cross as the cross of St Andrew's crucifixion. I want now to discuss in more detail the context in which this might have happened, and, in the course of this enquiry, to relate arguments about time and place and authority to the speculations I have advanced about why this fundamental change in iconography occurred.

We have seen that the earliest representations of the saint on the X cross so far authenticated come from the early to mid twelfth century. They are the Cottam font and the Ickleton wall painting in England, and the Quercy capital from France. I should remind the reader that in none of these cases is the figure actually named as St Andrew, but I am confident that the attribution is right. In particular I feel the details of the carving of the Quercy capital make the identification in that case secure. The exact provenance of this capital is not known; there is nothing to link it with a major religious establishment. In fact all these pieces seem to come from unimportant places, which makes it improbable that any of them was actually the first ever instance of this image of the saint. It is past credit to believe that a rather freakish innovative decision, made, say, by a school of local sculptors in Yorkshire, could have set a fashion that then swept the country. Surely the first appearance of St Andrew on an X-shaped cross must have been at some major Christian centre of cult? Where is this likely to have been?

I have maintained throughout this book that I believe the X cross originated in Britain. However, we must start from the early Quercy capital, and that means thinking first of France as a possibility. But it seems to me improbable that the development was there. I say this because of the evidence from sculpture at the great French cathedrals. I wrote earlier that the figures of apostles shown on the fine doorways of these churches, starting with Chartres, and continuing with others like Amiens and Rheims, begin from about 1200 to be carved carrying the symbols of their martyrdoms. In these sculptures St Andrew is shown carrying a cross, but it is an upright, Latin, one. At this date no one at these great centres of worship and art in France thought of giving St Andrew an X-shaped cross. This fits in with all the other evidence as to the saint's iconography on the Continent in the twelfth and early thirteenth centuries.

We are left with the Quercy capital as an anomaly but, as I wrote earlier, there may have been some special reason why the sculptor followed a developing British fashion rather than current French practice. (There were strong links between England and south-west France in the twelfth century; in 1152 Eleanor of Aquitaine was married to the man who became Henry II of England, ruler therefore of both lands.) That the capital should be dated even earlier than the Cottam font does not present a special difficulty in that I am not supposing the font was in fact the earliest example of the X cross in Britain.

In Britain we have nothing like the surviving wealth of figurative sculpture of the Romanesque period that there is in France and Spain, and, as I have written earlier, I do not know of any actual carving of St Andrew, with or without a cross, between AD 800 or so and the Cottam font in the mid twelfth century. More and more early wall paintings in English churches are being discovered and restored; so far the earliest seems to be the one at Ickleton, also of the twelfth century.

Andrew has always been a popular saint in England, with many church dedications in his name. A lot of these, however, are of course small village churches and I suppose we should expect to look primarily to the more important centres of Andrew's cult for evidence of developments in his iconography such as could have had widespread and lasting influence. I think especially of Wilfrid's church at Hexham, of the cathedrals of Rochester and Peterborough, and of the church at Wells. This was an early Andrew foundation but it had a long

and chequered history, which culminated in 1245 in recognition as a 'cathedral', as seat of a bishop, that is – but jointly with
Bath Abbey. But there is little in fact or story at these places to
give positive support to the idea that the X-shaped cross was
invented at one or other of these churches.

We saw that many moderns believe there was a link between
St Andrews and Hexham, and that relics were brought north
from the church there, but this is only speculation. There is
nothing, I think, now at Hexham or in its records that has
bearing on the early iconography of St Andrew. Nor are there
artefacts at Rochester Cathedral – other than the seals I have
discussed, which are interesting but not early enough to stand
out as significant. The same seems to be true of the material
associated with Peterborough.

As for Bath and Wells, the seals with 'saltires', which I
described in the last chapter, are perhaps worth more investigation. There are also the two early, eleventh-century, capitals at Bath, of which one at least has usually been identified as
showing St Vincent (see p. 65–7). In itself this representation
could not have been understood as showing torture or martyrdom on anything like an X-shaped cross, and I do not think we
can consider that it could possibly have played any role in the
genesis of the idea that *St Andrew* died on such a cross. It is, I
suppose, possible that the cult of St Vincent somewhere in
Britain involved depiction of him hanging on a Y- or X-shaped
structure, which might have led to misinterpretation, but the
earliest example that I know of is the (likely but not certain)
portrayal of this saint in a window in York Minster, and that
dates to the early fourteenth century.

We are clutching at straws here, I am afraid. And I cannot
think of other ecclesiastical sites in England which would
promise us more. What about Scotland, and St Andrews itself?

Here there was a centre of cult and pilgrimage, attracting
a wide range of visitors even by the time of Queen Margaret who
died in 1093. Its importance and prosperity were much enhanced
by the introduction of Augustinian canons, a virtual refounding of
the Establishment, favoured by King Alexander I, who died in
1124, and completed by 1144, under his successor David I.

The coming of the Augustinians marked a break in worship, in organisation and in church building. We saw that one version of the old Pictish legend of the institution of the cult of St Andrew on the Fife site was recorded by an Augustinian canon who lived in the time of David I. This canon goes on to write very disparagingly of the religious situation which the Augustinians found at St Andrews, and one indication of the new order is the way in which Pictish Christian artefacts, fine crosses and other sculpture, were thrown away, buried or used as building material by the new masters. Did anything of the old traditions survive?

Now in earlier chapters we have noticed two devices which might conceivably have led to misunderstanding and the belief that St Andrew died on an X-shaped cross, and which are images which merit particular discussion in a Scottish context. I refer to the chi-rho, and to the 'saltires' on St Andrews seals. Could it be that something in the artistic and ecclesiastical record of St Andrews itself led to the 'invention' of the X cross?

We saw that a chi-rho figured in the dedication of the Church of St Paul at Jarrow, dated to AD 685, and I put forward the suggestion that such a device might have been also used in the consecration of the Church of St Peter which King Nechtan of the Picts asked builders from Northumbria to erect in his kingdom in AD 710. Might a chi-rho then have been inscribed at a church of St Andrew in Pictland a generation or so later? I also wrote of the possible influence on Pictish kings of traditions about the Emperor Constantine the Great, and suggested that King Angus might have used a chi-rho as a battle standard device. Could there have been examples in the Pictish and later Scottish material which were then misunderstood, with the passage of time or with the changes in Church organisation and control which St Andrews experienced?

It is worth remembering that the chi-rho in its original, 'Roman', form – the form in which it is not over-fanciful to see a possibility of misinterpretation, as a man on a cross – did not continue to be regularly used in Britain. I do not in fact know of any actual surviving example in Scotland, and certainly not at St Andrews. But although there is no positive material evidence from St Andrews to give weight to the theory that a misinterpreted chi-ro figure there could have given rise to the idea of the X-shaped cross, I think it is worth retaining it as a possibility.

We have seen that early seals of St Andrews Priory did have a device of an X shape, but that it is at least questionable whether we should interpret this as intended to represent a cross of crucifixion, at least originally. A problem I have already mentioned is that it does seem unlikely that the symbol, needing to be understood as that of St Andrew's cross, should be used by the Church before there was any practice of representing the saint on or with such a cross. The seals themselves, of course, belong to the period of 'Augustinian' control, but I suppose it would be possible to argue that the device was used because it was already familiar at St Andrews and was something that the Augustinians took over from the earlier Church. Could it have figured on an early reliquary – whether it signified there 'the cross' (as Christian symbol) or 'bones'?

If indeed the Augustinians found it when they came to St Andrews, and in whatever context they found it, what significance would they have given to it? Did they simply use it, as so often artistic devices are used, without consciousness of conveying an old meaning or intention to convey a new one? Was it only later that this X shape on the seals would have been interpreted as St Andrew's special cross of crucifixion (as it largely is today)? A relevant question of course is, what did the Augustinians in the mid twelfth century themselves believe about the death of St Andrew?

An important point to get clear is that it cannot have been simply a 'new' misunderstanding of the device actually on these seals – the earliest we have was produced in about 1180 – which gave birth to the idea that St Andrew had a special cross, for the seals are not early enough to account for the representations of the saint so martyred on the Cottam font and on the Quercy capital.

Suppose that we argue that either the 'saltire' device (perhaps on a reliquary representing bones) or a chi-rho figure, had already come to be misinterpreted at St Andrews as a cross of crucifixion in the twelfth, even the eleventh, century, well before the Augustinians came there? Could the church in St Andrews, and the pilgrims visiting it, have been responsible for spreading down south the new idea about the saint's death, for it to emerge in a place like Cottam in England, and indeed in Quercy in France, by 1140 or so? Is it credible to believe that such a momentous development in what became the accepted story of the saint was achieved by the remote and then relatively unimportant outpost of Christendom in Fife?

In considering this theory we have to admit that there are no artefacts actually found at St Andrews which show the saint on or with the X cross from the period before the coming of the Augustinians. However we have to remind ourselves of the paucity of surviving evidence and its nature. For example, Gamelin may have been the first bishop to use a seal showing St Andrew on the X cross, but it seems to have been only in the mid thirteenth century that *saints* began to be generally shown on British ecclesiastical seals. Bishops at St Andrews before Gamelin, even clerics of the pre-Augustinian church there, might have been familiar with the X-shaped cross as that of Andrew's martyrdom, and actually had or commissioned pictorial images of this in some form, which have simply not survived.

One disturbing thing is that we have to accept that those 'saltires' on seals, which may have been derived originally from some image of a cross-symbol or of bones, not of a cross of crucifixion at all, continued to be reproduced for centuries with no attempt to modify them to make them more like the cross of St Andrew, as it is shown where there is undoubted reference to his death. But this is a problem anyway!

Another rather puzzling thing is that the versions of the legend about the foundation of St Andrews say nothing about the saint having a special form of cross, although one of them does refer to the 'cross of Christ' seen in the sky. Neither was the Augustinian canon, who, after giving Version B of the foundation legend, wrote about the early worship of St Andrew at the site, drawn to writing anything about the manner of the saint's death. Did he and his contemporaries – did the Picts before them – think St Andrew died on an ordinary Latin cross, and was it only later, though certainly by the time of Bishop Gamelin, that the idea of the X-shaped cross was adopted in St Andrews, perhaps taken over from some practice in England?

It is possible to imagine that there was something at St Andrews – a chi-rho or some other misunderstood 'X' shape – which led to the 'invention' of the X-shaped cross at this site. It has to be conceded however that there is no concrete evidence for this. Nothing positively requires us to place such an idea and such an image at St Andrews earlier than those thirteenth-century seals, starting with that of Bishop Gamelin, which actually portray the saint on such a cross. And these seals are no earlier than seals from places in England such as Rochester and Wells.

The reader may want to argue that perhaps the Augus-tinians did not find the idea of the saint's death on an X-shaped cross already in vogue at St Andrews, but brought it with them. Where they got it from – the actual origin and inspiration of the idea – would have to be left as a mystery. This question, however, might start another line of enquiry. I have been writing about some particular ecclesiastical sites as the source from which the idea of the X-shaped cross might have spread. It might be fruitful to consider religious orders (or even the careers of particular churchmen? or artists or craftsmen?) as the channel through which this new way of thinking of the death of St Andrew, once it had come into being, could have been popularised. An enquiry on these lines might also lead to suggestions as to how and why the idea of the X-shaped cross could have originated – either in a misinterpretation of some image or even possibly because of some doctrinal speculation – in such a setting or with such individuals.

As it is, I have devoted considerable space to examining St Andrews' particular claim to be the place where the X-shaped cross was adopted, linking this to two of the theories I outlined earlier, theories which I thought might account for such an association of the saint and the X. The result has been, to say the least, inconclusive. And I doubt whether, in the present state of our knowledge any attempt to build on one or the other of those theories, or to connect the development with some other specific British site, would yield anything more convincing. We need to discover more evidence!

# *In Conclusion*

My last chapter has been disconcertingly full of question marks. We do not seem any nearer deciding exactly where the X-shaped cross of St Andrew originated, or why. This may seem a disappointing conclusion. I had hoped myself that one trail or another would lead to something more than speculation, to some seriously plausible theory as to the origin of the idea. As it is, if I am asked which lines of enquiry seem to me to emerge as most promising I would suggest two, rather different, possibilities. Was it that depictions of the death of St Andrew spread-eagled on a tree were misinterpreted as showing death on an X-shaped cross? Or was it that some symbol in an X-shape – bones, or a cross of faith, or a chi-rho – which was associated with the honouring of St Andrew, was misunderstood as a symbol of a special cross of crucifixion?

I do indeed hope that this study will encourage others to investigate further these and other questions raised concerning the association of the X cross with St Andrew, and the origins of the saltire.

# Bibliography

## A. General

*PG* = Migne, J.P., *Patrologia Graeca* (Paris 1856–66)

*PL* = Migne, J.P., *Patrologia Latina* (Paris 1844–64)

Ash, M. and Broun, D., 'The Adoption of St Andrew as Patron Saint of Scotland', in Higgitt, J. (ed.), *Medieval Art and Architecture in the Diocese of St Andrews* (Leeds 1994), pp. 16–24

Borst, A., 'Patron Saints in Medieval Society', in *Medieval Worlds: Barbarians, Heretics and Artists in the Middle Ages* (Cambridge 1991), pp. 125–44

Hall, U., 'St Andrew the Apostle' in *New Dictionary of National Biography* (Oxford 2004)

Hall, U., *St Andrew and Scotland* (St Andrews 1994)

Hannay, R.K., *Saint Andrew of Scotland* (Edinburgh 1934)

Peterson, P., *Andrew, the Brother of Simon Peter*, suppl. vol. 1 (1958) of *Novum Testamentum*

Pneumatikakis, C., Ο Πρωτοκλητος Αποστολος Ανδρεας (Athens 1971)

Turnbull, M.T.R.B., *Saint Andrew* (Edinburgh 1997)

## B. The Literary Tradition Concerning the Saints

The most comprehensive general collection of material on the saints is the ongoing publication, *Acta Sanctorum*, by the Bollandists, with texts and discussion in Latin. Saints are included under their festal dates and I have given references in my text to material relating to several individuals. 'Andrew the Apostle' has not yet been covered, as publication is proceeding through the months and has not reached his festal day, 30 November.

Beleth, J., *De Ecclesiasticis Officiis*, Corpus Christianorum, Continuatio Mediaevalis, vol. 41a (Turnhout 1976)

Elliott, J.K., *The Apocryphal New Testament* (Oxford 1993), based on James, M.R., *The Apocryphal New Testament* (Oxford 1924, 1953)

Lipsius R.A. and Bonnet, M., *Acta Apostolorum Apocrypha*. vol. 2,1 (Leipzig 1898; Darmstadt 1959) contains texts in Greek and Latin concerning St Andrew.

Roze, J.B.M., *La Légende Dorée* (Paris 1902)

Schermann, T., *Prophetarum Vitae Fabulosae Indices Apostolorum Discipulorumque Domini* (Leipzig 1907), for brief early references to St Andrew and his martyrdom

Schneemelcher, W. (ed.), *New Testament Apocrypha*, English trans. By Wilson, R. McL., 2 vols. (Cambridge and Louisville 1991, 1992)

Voragine, Jacobus de, *Legenda Aurea*, English trans. in Ryan, W.G., *The Golden Legend*, 2 vols. (Princeton 1993)


## C. The Tradition Concerning St Andrew

*Andreas*, modern English version in Bradley, S.A.J., *Anglo-Saxon Poetry* (London 1982)

Gregory of Tours, *Liber de Miraculis Beati Andreae Apostoli*, in *Monumenta Germaniae Historica, Scriptores Rerum Merovingicarum*, vol. 1, pt. 1 (Hanover 1885). Text in Latin. In Latin and French in Prieur, below

Prieur, J.M., *Acta Andreae*, vols. 5 and 6 of Corpus Christianorum, Series Apocryphorum (Turnhout 1989). Texts, with translations and discussion in French.

Cross, S.H. and Sherbowitz-Wetzor, O.P., *The Russian Primary Chronicle* (Cambridge, MA 1953), pp. 53–4 on St Andrew.

Dvornik, F., *The Idea of Apostolicity in Byzantium and the Legend of the Apostle Andrew* (Dumbarton Oaks Studies, 4) (Cambridge, MA 1958)

MacDonald, D.R., *Christianizing Homer. The Odyssey, Plato and the Acts of Andrew* (New York 1994)


## D. St Andrew in the Scottish Tradition

Blew, W. (ed.), *Breviarium Aberdonense*, Bannatyne Club, vol. 96 (London 1854), first section, fol. 131–2; second section, fol. 1–13, 82–3, 96. In Latin

Boece, H., *Scotorum Historiae* (Paris 1527). In English in *Holinshed's Chronicles of England, Scotland and Ireland* (London 1807–8), vol. 5

Bower, W., *Scotichronicon*, general ed. Watt, D. (Aberdeen 1990– )

Metcalfe, W.M., *Legends of the Scottish Saints*, Scottish Tracts Society, vol. 13 (Edinburgh 1896)

Skene, W. (ed.), *Chronicles of the Picts, Chronicles of the Scots and Other Early Memorials of Scottish History* (Edinburgh 1967) For versions of the St Andrews foundation legend, in Latin.


## E. Christianity and the Cult of St Andrew in England and Scotland

Bede, Hymns attributed to, in Corpus Christianorum, Series Latina, vol. 122 (Turnhout 1955)

Bede, *Ecclesiastical History of the English People*, trans. by Sherley-Price, L. (London 1955, 1990)

Eddius, 'Life of Wilfrid', trans. by Webb, J.F. and Farmer, D.H. in *The Age of Bede* (London 1988)

Bond, F. *Dedications and Patron Saints of English Churches* (London 1914)

Duncan, A.A.M., *Scotland: The Making of the Kingdom* (Edinburgh 1975)

Forster, F.A. *Studies in Church Dedications* (London 1899)
MacKinlay, J.M. *Ancient Church Dedications in Scotland* (Edinburgh 1910)
McQueen, J. and W., *St Nynia* (Edinburgh 2005)
Smyth, A.P. *Warlords and Holy Men* (Edinburgh 1984)
Thomas, C. *Christianity in Roman Britain* (London 1981)
Thomas, C. *The Early Christian Archaeology of North Britain* (London 1971)
Walsh, M.M., 'St Andrew in Anglo-Saxon England' in *Annuale Mediaevale* 20 (1981), 97–122


## F. Burgundian Traditions

Olivier de la Marche, *Mémoires,* pub. by Société de l'Histoire de France (Paris 1883)
Cockshaw, P. *L'Ordre de la Toisson d'Or* (Brussels 1996)
Maduère, Pidoux de la, 'L'apôtre Saint-André, Patron des Bourguignons', *Bulletin de l'Académie des Sciences . . . de Besançon* (1935), 66–101
Seeck, O. *Notitia Dignitatum* (Paris 1876, Frankfurt am Main 1962)


## G. Iconography – General

Braunfels, W. and Kirschbaum, E., *Lexikon der Christliche Ikonographie*, vol. 5 *Ikonographie der Heiligen* (Freiburg 1973)
Kaftal, G. *Iconography of the Saints in Central and South Italian Painting* (Florence 1986)
Kaftal, G. *Iconography of the Saints in the Painting of North East Italy* (Florence 1978)
Kaftal, G. *Iconography of the Saints in Tuscan Painting* (Florence 1952)
Kingsley Porter, A. *Romanesque Sculpture of the Pilgrimage Roads* (Boston 1923, New York 1965–85)
Lasko, P., *Ars Sacra* (New Haven, Conn. 1994)
Réau, L., *Iconographie de l'Art Chretien*, vol. 3.1 for St Andrew (Paris 1958)
Rohault de Fleury, C. and G., *Archéologie Chrétienne. Les Saints de la Messe et leur Monuments*, vol. 10 for St Andrew (Paris 1900)
Sauerländer, W., trans. Sondheimer, J. *Gothic Sculpture in France 1170–1240* (London 1972)
Seroux d'Agincourt, J.B.L.G., *Histoire de l'Art par les Monuments* (Paris 1823)


## H. Iconography – St Andrew in Particular

Alexander, J. and Binski, P. (eds), *Age of Chivalry* (London 1987). For the Ulrick frontal
Cahn, W., *Romanesque Sculpture in American Collections*, vol. 2 (Turnhout 1999). For the Quercy capital at Bryn Athyn
Geijer, A., *Textile Treasures of Uppsala Cathedral* (Stockholm 1964). For the Uppsala cope
Mâle, E., 'Histoire et Légende de l'Apôtre Saint André dans l'Art' *Revue des Deux Mondes* 19 (1951), 412–20
Pillinger, R., *Der Apostel Andreas*, monograph 612, *Öst. Ak. Der Wiss.* (Vienna 1994)

## I. Art and Images in Britain

Birch, W. de G., *Catalogue of Seals in the Department of Manuscripts in the British Museum* (London 1887)

Bond, F., *Fonts and Font-covers* (Oxford 1908)

Calvert, T. 'The Iconography of the St Andrew Auckland Cross' *Art Bulletin* 66 (1984), 543–55

Christie, A.G.I., *English Medieval Embroidery* (Oxford 1938)

Cramp, R. *Corpus of Anglo-Saxon Stone Sculpture*, vols. 1 and 2 *Durham and Northumberland* (Oxford 1984)

Henderson, G. and I. *The Art of the Picts* (London 2004)

Mann, F., *Early Medieval Church Sculpture: A Study of 12$^{th}$ Century Fragments in East Yorkshire* (Cherry Burton 1985). For the Cottam font

Nelson, P., *Ancient Painted Glass in England* (London 1913)

Park, D., 'Romanesque Wall Paintings at Ickleton', in *Romanesque and Gothic: Essays for George Zarnecki* (Woodbridge 1987)

Pedrick, G. *Monastic Seals of the Thirteenth Century* (London 1902)

Stevenson, J.H. and Wood, M., *Scottish Heraldic Seals* (Glasgow 1940)

Tristram, E.W., *English Medieval Wall-Painting. The Thirteenth Century* (London 1950)

Yeoman, P., *Pilgrimage in Medieval Scotland* (London 1999)


## J. Crucifixion, the Cross, the Chi-Rho

Braun, J. *Der Christliche Altar* (Munich 1924), pp. 441–2, 460–1. For the Trier reliquary

Browne, T., *The Garden of Cyrus*, in *Religio Medici and Other Works*, ed. Martin, L.C. (Oxford 1964)

Cabrol, P. and others, *Dictionnaire d'Archéologie Chrétienne et de Liturgie* (Paris 1907–53)

Durandus, W., *Rationale Divinorum Officiorum* – Book 1 translated in Neale, J.M. and Weble, B., *The Symbolism of Churches and Church Ornaments* (London 1893)

Jones, A.H.M., *Constantine and the Conversion of Europe* (London 1948)

Kent, J.P.C., *Roman Coins* (London 1978)

Lipsius, J. *De Cruce*, in *Opera Omnia*, vol. 3 (Antwerp 1637)

Middleton, J.H., 'On consecration crosses, with some English examples', *Archeologia* 48.2 (1885),

Mommsen, Th. *Römisches Strafrecht* (Leipzig 1899)

Robinson, J., *The Lewis Chessmen* (London 2004)

Stuart, J. *The Sculptured Stones of Scotland* (Aberdeen, 1856–7)

# Index

*Index*